Women without Men

By Donald J. Greiner

The Notebook of Stephen Crane (editor)

Comic Terror:
  The Novels of John Hawkes

Robert Frost:
  The Poet and His Critics

American Poets since World War II:
  Ammons through Kumin (editor)

American Poets since World War II:
  Levertov through Zukofsky (editor)

The Other John Updike:
  Poems / Short Stories / Prose / Play

John Updike's Novels

Adultery in the American Novel:
  Updike, James, Hawthorne

Understanding John Hawkes

Domestic Particulars:
  The Novels of Frederick Busch

Women Enter the Wilderness:
  Male Bonding and the American Novel of the 1980s

Women without Men:
  Female Bonding and the American Novel of the 1980s

WOMEN
without
MEN

Female Bonding and
the American Novel of the 1980s

DONALD J. GREINER

University of South Carolina Press

For Ellen,
as always, and for
five colleagues in American literature
who have helped me throughout my career:
Matthew J. Bruccoli
David Cowart
James Dickey
Benjamin Franklin V
Joel Myerson

Copyright © 1993 University of South Carolina

Published in Columbia, South Carolina, by the
University of South Carolina Press

Manufactured in the United States of America

Library of Congress Cataloging-in-Publication Data

Greiner, Donald J.
   Women without men : female bonding and the American novel of the
1980s / Donald J. Greiner.
     p. cm.
   Includes bibliographical references (p.) and index.
   ISBN 0-87249-884-0 (acid-free paper)
   1. American fiction—20th century—History and criticism.
   2. Women and literature—United States—History—20th century.
   3. American fiction—Women authors—History and criticism.
   4. Femininity (Psychology) in literature. 5. Friendship in
literature. I. Title.
PS374.W6G74 1993
813'.5409352042—dc20

Contents

Acknowledgments

Acknowledgments are a pleasure to write. Professor Bert Dillon, chair of the Department of English at the University of South Carolina, was always supportive. Carol Cutsinger typed the entire manuscript. My graduate assistant, Mary Katzif, tracked down fugitive bibliographical information and checked primary sources with energy and good humor. Amy Hudock read one of the chapters on feminist theory to make sure that I was not too far astray. Eric Roman used his expertise with the computer to help me with the list of sources. One of my most helpful colleagues, Professor Benjamin Franklin V, read parts of the manuscript and listened patiently as I discussed some of the ideas. My greatest debts are to Professor David Cowart of the University of South Carolina and to Professor Susan Strehle of the State University of New York–Binghamton for reading the entire manuscript and for debating the issues sympathetically and constructively. Both were ideal readers. With this book I have climbed out on a limb yet again, but these colleagues have kept me from falling.

Women without Men

Chapter One

Introduction: Female Bonding and Cultural Controversy

I didn't want to be pegged as the mother-daughter expert.

—Amy Tan to Mervyn Rothstein,
New York Times, 11 June 1991

The history of women has been seriously affected by the history of the novel.

—Rachel M. Brownstein,
Becoming a Heroine: Reading about Women in Novels

Men without Women

—Ernest Hemingway, 1927

My goals in this book are to investigate the complexities of female bonding as delineated in a series of contemporary novels by women and to discuss the variations as significant alternatives to important changes brought to American literature by recent male novelists. Because I have been warned by feminist colleagues, who nevertheless have been steadfast in their support of my work, I am well aware that my position as a white, middle-class, Anglo-Saxon male might persuade some readers to dismiss my analyses of novels by women. I can only respond with the hope that such a parochial reaction is not the case. A study of contemporary fiction by women, *Women without Men: Female Bonding and the American Novel of the 1980s* grew out of questions I asked but did not answer in the concluding remarks of another book I wrote recently. Entitled *Women Enter the Wilderness: Male Bonding and the American Novel of the 1980s*, the book argued that a radical change had occurred in contemporary novels written by men.[1] Focusing on such authors as Frederick Busch (*Sometimes I Live in the Country*, 1986)

1

John Irving (*A Prayer for Owen Meany*, 1989), Padgett Powell (*Edisto*, 1984), Richard Russo (*The Risk Pool*, 1988), and Larry Woiwode (*Born Brothers*, 1988) among others, I discussed how these writers had revised the paradigm of canonical American fiction that links James Fenimore Cooper through Melville and Twain to Hemingway, Faulkner, and Dickey. The paradigm—allowing for significant variations, of course—is simply stated: males in American literature first bond and then cross the border between society and the wilderness in order to quest toward the freedom of adventure by leaving females behind. There is nothing new in this observation. Such commentators as D. H. Lawrence, R. W. B. Lewis, and Leslie Fiedler have all but codified the paradigm in the critical theory that informs much of the analysis of American literature.

What *is* new—and remarkably so—is that contemporary fiction by males indicates a primary shift in the canon. Males still bond in the novels cited above, and they still cross the river to enter the trees, but they reject the mandate to leave women behind. Indeed, the men in these contemporary novels either take the woman with them on the quest or find her already there. To show why and how the change occurred, in *Women Enter the Wilderness* I analyzed theories of male bonding from the perspectives of both biodeterminist anthropologists and the feminist anthropologists who dispute them. According to the former, as articulated notably by Lionel Tiger and Robin Fox, male bonding is a biological imperative developed in the early eons of the species to exploit the aggressiveness of man-the-hunter in protecting the tribe (society).[2] Feminist scholars, especially Ruth Bleier and Donna J. Haraway,[3] reject theories of bonding which stress biology and argue, instead, that traditions of culture shape behavior and gender.

The male bonds of Leatherstocking-Chingachgook, Ishmael-Queequeg, and Huck-Jim are so inviolate that they have attained the status of literary and cultural myth. One does not easily forget that Chingachgook always guards Natty's back, that Ishmael survives on Queequeg's coffin, that Huck will "go to hell" for Jim. Similarly, a male bond that is invincible and all but eternal informs such twentieth-century novels of the masculine quest as Faulkner's *Go Down, Moses* (1942) and Dickey's *Deliverance* (1970). Male novelists of the 1980s document the impulse to bond, but they offer the unexpected variation of women being included in a tie between men which holds firm and true.

Such reconciliation of the genders may not be the case, however, in contemporary novels by women, and in this study I want to ask why. Susan K. Harris suggests an answer in her analysis of differences between nineteenth-century American women's fiction and novels of the male adventure which have traditionally defined the canon. Acknowledging that canonical male fiction values the individual over society, Harris observes: "In contemporary women's texts, on the other hand, the basic thematic is less self against society than self against self; that is, the women's internal conflicts represent conflicting definitions of womanhood. The characters battle themselves far more often, and with greater intensity, than they engage an openly corrupt society."[4] Harris's point is well taken, but I suspect that the issue of female bonding in contemporary novels by women involves other equally interesting complexities. To suggest the extent of the problem I recapitulate the concluding remarks of *Women Enter the Wilderness*, remarks in which I cite Marianne Wiggins and Gloria Naylor as illustrations.

I

The problem is as difficult to solve as it is easy to state: Biodeterminists would have one believe that females do not bond. Lionel Tiger summarizes their position: "In both violent and aggressive action male bonding is the predominant instrument of organization. Females tend to be excluded from aggressive organizations. . . . They do not form groups which are expressly devoted to violent activity or to potentially violent action."[5] Anthropological evidence cited in feminist studies of primate and human behavior questions Tiger's claim. So does contemporary literary evidence. An examination of two novels published in the 1980s, Marianne Wiggins's *John Dollar* (1989) and Gloria Naylor's *The Women of Brewster Place* (1982), suggests that females bond as readily as males. They bond in varying degrees in *John Dollar* and *The Women of Brewster Place*, despite Tiger's assertion, but, unlike what happens in *A Prayer for Owen Meany* or *Born Brothers*, they do not rely on the opposite sex to secure the bond. The reasons may be political as well as anthropological.

The relationship between biodeterminist anthropology and contemporary fiction is as troublesome on the subject of female bonding as on the matter of man-the-hunter. In *The Woman That Never Evolved*, for example, Sarah Blaffer Hrdy confronts the issue directly.[6] A feminist sociobiologist—a term that many would deem an oxymoron—Hrdy disputes both feminists who believe that biological investigation is antifemale and biodeterminists who insist that the development of human society depended primarily on male bonding. The reader may question studies that, like Hrdy's, extrapolate conclusions about human potential from observations of primate behavior, but the point here is that Hrdy rejects Tiger's opinion that women do not bond. Indeed, she implies that the work of Tiger and other biodeterminists is obsolete. Based on her research in primatology, she argues that females participate in such supposedly male activities as competition and bonding: "selection favored females who were assertive, sexually active, or highly competitive, who adroitly manipulated male consorts, or who were as strongly motivated to gain high social status as they were to hold and carry babies" (14). One of Hrdy's significant conclusions is that female primates bond but that they do so "imperfectly" because they cooperate selfishly in an atmosphere of competition (100). Competition among females is well documented for every species of primate except the human, yet Hrdy demonstrates that not the absence of a competitive urge but the means of measuring it is the problem.

The tension between selfishness and cooperation in an environment of competition is a central concern in *John Dollar*.[7] Female bonding in Wiggins's novel is so fraught with violence and aggression as to make Tiger's comment questionable. Clearly indebted to *Lord of the Flies*, and frequently alluding to *Robinson Crusoe* and "The Rime of the Ancient Mariner" in order to heighten the atmosphere of savagery, *John Dollar* details the fate of a group of British schoolgirls left on an island without adult supervision after a tidal wave destroys the trappings of traditional authority. The novel may be read as both political commentary and religious parable because the girls are on the island for matters of empire and because allusions to the ritual of Holy Communion direct the climax. Wiggins reportedly considered titling the book *Eucharist*.[8] But my concern is with the matter of female bonding in a contemporary novel written by a woman about women and yet named for a man. For, despite the importance of John Dollar as the exemplar of passion, knowledge, and ironic spirituality, the ostensible main character is a female. Young, "unsexed" Charlotte Lewes, a World War I widow, exchanges phallocentric discourse for what the narrator calls "Sudden Loss of Language" when she abandons dormant England for mysterious Rangoon. Dollar reawakens her to sex, an activity for which words are unnecessary, but Wiggins's primary interest in the gender relationships of *John Dollar* focuses on the bonded schoolgirls and the man they will devour during a celebration of the Eucharist.

Wiggins frames the complexities of bonding with the paradoxes of patriarchy. Apparently abandoned on "the Island of Our Outlawed Dreams" after paying homage to King George, the royal figure of fatherhood, the eight females believe that they must reestablish patriarchal order if they are to survive. Thus, they write laws, rename objects, and honor authority—but these traditional staples of human society quickly disintegrate in the absence of male power. The girls' trek beyond the border to the territory of unknown vision forces them to bond in the aggressive manner that Hrdy affirms and Tiger denies, but Wiggins suggests that women-without-men is as sterile as its counterpart. Charlotte uses Dollar to reawaken into life. The girls literally feast on Dollar in order to live, but their ironic worship at a fleshly communion shrinks the bond. Wiggins's investigation of the link between aggression and bonding says as much about Otherness as any novel by an American male.

   John Dollar is a flashback, beginning with Charlotte's death as an old woman, but it soon turns to the island nightmare decades ago when she had "died before." Wiggins creates an air of endless menace as she details the bond between Charlotte and the younger woman called Monkey, who has cared for her from the time of the earlier "death." An Indian, an outsider, and an Other, Monkey is a female of a different race and, thus, the literary equivalent of Chingachgook, Queequeg, and Jim. Memory and silence form the center of her life with Charlotte: "They lost their religion to silence, they lost their forbearance to fear. Year after year they refused to forget, to look forward, look inward, look anywhere, but to sea" (5). Their experience with masculine power as illustrated in the arrogance of colonialism and the devotion to King George has made them leery of words. Most males, as Wiggins characterizes them in *John Dollar,* are devourers who make "one law for men . . . one law for women" (7). Associating males with such verbs of consumption as *eats, chews,* and *buries,* she sets the foundation for an irony that becomes apparent only when the bonded schoolgirls feed on paralyzed John Dollar in a perversion of religious renewal. Erotic undertones and mystical obsession combine in Wiggins's dismantling of patriarchy. But not all males are a menace. Wiggins's irony turns on the realization that Dollar is a life giver at different extremes for Charlotte and the girls and that Charlotte kills the two females who destroy the sustaining male. In Wiggins's piercing description of gender Charlotte is one of those "women who will try to cling on paper legs to the primeval" (10). She is a female who remembers love.

   Love transforms Charlotte in the wilderness because she accepts unfamiliar Burma as a locale in which England is only a myth, "a place more real in microcosm, in its re-creation, than in any actuality" (21). Wiggins's strong female adapts to circumstances beyond the border. Rather than seek male protection, she repudiates patriarchy by rejecting conventional language. That is, Wiggins shows Charlotte re-shaping her sense of self by reassembling words to signify objects in the territory which the English language cannot describe. She longs to live, writes Wiggins, outside "the King's Own Version of the text" (30). Her insistence on redefining life, objects, and language itself convinces the Burmese of her androgyny when they speak of her as "half-man half-woman" (23). More important, Charlotte illustrates Hrdy's conclusions about females selecting male partners. Having lost her husband in a war, the ultimate extension of male power, Charlotte surfaces from lassitude as soon as she chooses John Dollar for her lover. As if satirizing Cooper's obsession with bloodlines, Wiggins shows her female pathfinder in the wilderness dismissing received notions of "the Empire's racial purity" when Charlotte takes Dollar despite his unknown origins (24). In Cooper parlance she is eager to be a woman with a cross. Dollar's commitment to the discipline of reading reverses Charlotte's rejection of language, and, thus, Wiggins celebrates a crea-tive bond that blends race and gender. Similar affiliations are either negated or neglected in the canonical American novel. One wonders, then, whether the inadvertent dissolution of their bond following the girls' dismantling of Dollar persuades Charlotte reluctantly to abandon her ideal attachment of male-female and withdraw to the silence of the female bond with brown-skinned Monkey.

Such dilemmas are not resolved in *John Dollar*. Wiggins resists the simple formulas of gender politics and explores instead the ambiguities of relationships when males and females, adults and children, are swept ashore to a locale beyond law and statute. One also suspects that Wiggins wrote *John Dollar* as the other side of *Lord of the Flies*, as a literary-anthropological protest to show that women do bond, that women are aggressive, and that such matters are not always felicitous for either males or females. Men exhibit colonialist presumptuousness while planning to rename the Island of Our Outlawed Dreams as King George's Island, and girls, like Golding's boys, collapse to violence once law is wasted in the wilderness of what the narrator calls "an alien and purposeless reality" (158). As Hrdy argues and Wiggins confirms, females bond "imperfectly" because they react selfishly when placed in an environment of competition. Charlotte is Wiggins's exception. Longing to be outside the King's text, she pursues experience that bears "a likeness to the fictions that one's dreamed" (69). Distortion of the fiction precipitates her lapse from language toward silence.

The irony is that the girls become their own menacing Indians once traditional language breaks down. Decorating their faces with paint and feathers, watching Komodo dragons slaughter spawning sea turtles, and finding a human skull that apparently has been partly eaten, the young women metamorphose into the alien tribes that male American novelists have always pictured on the far side of the border. To conclude that "we have met the enemy and she is us" may be too neat, but Wiggins nevertheless suggests that the need to bond in dire circumstances and the perversion of the bond because of competitive violence are all but simultaneous impulses within each member of the group. She is much more skeptical than contemporary male writers. Once the tidal wave propels the girls to the land of outlawed dreams, where "no one was glad to discover that she was alive," they learn that their training to gather wood, construct houses, make fabric, mint money, invent wheels, name objects, and declaim laws as worthless (112). They believe that "to abjure the text" is to break the law, but, like James Dickey, Wiggins places her bonded companions in a territory in which the text is never read (121). Of the group, only Monkey, a modern-day Scheherazade with the texts of a hundred and one stories in her memory, survives.

With the girls' grotesque corruption of baptism, communion, and burial, Wiggins signals the final disintegration of the bond. John Dollar even compares the females to primates—chimpanzees—when he realizes that they have failed to organize their efforts at survival. They expect him to be God, the ultimate father, and tell them what to do. He expects them to be responsible human beings and make a concerted effort to live. Cannibalization of the male thwarts both expectations. John Dollar is no Natty Bumppo charging to the rescue to reassert the primacy of civilized male authority. Revising such assumptions of the traditional American novel, Wiggins describes the injured Dollar watching cannibals eat the girls' fathers (males killing males, as in Cooper and Dickey) and then suffering a similar fate himself when two girls partially devour him in a perversion of the Eucharist (females killing males, as in few other recent American fictions). Wiggins's final unexpected twist of the complex gender relationships in *John Dollar* occurs when Charlotte destroys the female bond by killing the two girls: females killing females, as an illustration of the imperfect bonding noted by Hrdy. "Theirs," writes Wiggins in a disturbing understatement, "is failure of community" (189). In her intertextual nod to *Lord of the Flies* bonds quickly disintegrate, and the wilderness always wins. Normalities of gender are finally irrelevant in the domain of unknown vision.

Gloria Naylor is less skeptical than Marianne Wiggins about the durability of female bonding. Female solidarity is the subject of *The Women of Brewster Place*, so much so that no male in the novel has even the limited strength of John Dollar. Fathers, husbands, lovers, sons—all are either violent or absent, as they tend to be also in Alice Walker's *The Color Purple* (1983). Naylor's men lead separate lives and do not bond. Usually patriarchal and always exploitative, they illustrate the dissolution of the black family because of the weakness of the black male. There is no Mr. O'Nolan *(Sometimes I Live in the Country)* or Wussy *(The Risk Pool)* to give sustenance and individual strength. More important, there is no bonding in *The Women of Brewster Place* between black and white males. An unsympathetic reader might argue that black O'Nolan and Wussy are idealistic projections by white, male authors, updated but nevertheless nostalgic recreations of Twain's Jim. Such skepticism does not concern Naylor in *The Women of Brewster Place*. Focusing on matriarchy, she writes about the widely perceived social phenomenon of the breakdown of the black family bond.

Feminist socioanthropologist Carol B. Stack disputes the phenomenon. A white scholar who conducted her research in a black urban community called The Flats, where she lived for three years, Stack published her findings in *All Our Kin: Strategies for Survival in a Black Community.*[9] In her analysis of the prevailing cultural stereotypes of poor blacks she challenges the conclusion that the "broken" black family unit, usually matriarchal, is "deviant." People within the group interpret their own circumstances differently from that of the norm. In Stack's words they rely on "collective expectations and obligations created by cooperative networks of poverty-stricken kinsmen" which foster a stability usually ignored by outsiders (24). The point is that poverty facilitates bonding. The result is a necessary sharing of goods and services among those within the bond. Given such a framework of attachments, the traditional definition of the family (husband, wife, children) is inadequate to account for the support networks in a black community. Stack found that she had to redefine *family* as "the smallest, organized, durable network of kin and non-kin who interact daily, providing domestic needs of children and assuring their survival" (31).

Nevertheless, in discussing "personal kindreds," a kind of extended family involving kin and nonkin, Stack shows that the young adult black male often avoids the commitment traditionally associated with family responsibility. Naylor uses literature to counter sociology, and she criticizes such male evasion of accountability in her portrait of Cora Lee and the men who exploit her. Both contribute to the disintegration of family bonding among blacks. Stack, however, distinguishes between the folk system and the legal system of parenthood. The latter is the conventional definition of kinship and dependability; the former is "those people who actively accept responsibility toward" the children (46). These people are usually female—grandmothers of young pregnant black women or else aunts and sisters—and they assume the duty of raising the child. Thus, the biological mother and the child's "mama" are not necessarily the same.

Fatherhood is a different issue: "very few women in The Flats are married before they have given birth to one or more children" (50). The chain of socially recognized relatives which exists through the mother and her extended kin does not commonly apply to the father. Stack found that a child is accepted into the loose bonding relationships of the father only if the father becomes "an immediate sponsor of a child's kinship network" (50). She also learned that the community will tolerate the male's denial of paternity, though she argues that "the pattern whereby black children derive all their kin through females has been stereotyped and exaggerated in the literature on black families" (51). Naylor might disagree. Her characterizations of black males in *The Women of Brewster Place* are entirely negative. The result is her celebration of women and of the aggressiveness of their bonds. From Stack's perspective the problem is environmental, because many black males lack the productive employment necessary to claim parental rights. If a male does little beyond acknowledging the child, he loses his rights: "the most important single factor which affects interpersonal relationships between men and women in The Flats is unemployment" (112). Stack's observation—devastating when fictionalized in *Brewster Place*—is that "mothers expect little from the father; they just hope that he will help out. But they do expect something from his kin, especially his mother and sisters" (53). Activating these "kin lines" through exchanges and dependencies constitutes "the main activity of daily life for these women" (53). Clearly, female bonding is a potent force.

This social phenomenon is the center of Naylor's novel, but she takes a much less sanguine position than Stack on the problem of the absent male. Stack insists that the children have "constant and close contact" with men, despite the "important role of the black female" (104). Naylor argues otherwise, though she would likely agree with Stack that, since black women usually control the finances, men do not hesitate to cheat women economically. Indeed, the need to avoid exploitation may be the reason for the female bond. Stack quotes the reaction of an unmarried mother: "The point is a woman has to have her own pride. She can't let a man rule her" (110). The result is that many poor black females debase males to the extent of regarding them as inherently "bad" and thereby reverse the traditional association of women and "the Fall." Faced with unstable gender relationships, the females bond together because they realize that welfare checks and kinship networks offer greater financial security than the unreliable male. Marriage merely deflects resources from the female bond. Fathers are not always absent, as popular lore would have it, but they do lack authority. Stack's conclusion illustrates the strength of female bonding: "Kin regard any marriage as both a risk to the woman and her children and as a threat to the durability of the kin group" (117). Little wonder that she writes in her final chapter about "the domestic authority of women, and limitations on the role of the husband or male friend within a woman's kin network" (124).

Male limitations are unrelenting in *The Women of Brewster Place*.[10] Late in the novel the narrator describes a gang of black adolescent thugs as "the most dangerous species in existence—human males with an erection to validate" (170). The ultimate perversion of man-the-hunter, these males are a horrifying degeneration of bonding. Aware that they will never be called on "to thrust a bayonet into an Asian farmer, target a torpedo . . . [or] point a finger to move a nation," they cling together as a pack in order to hunt the one animal they can dominate, the female (160). Naylor's graphic account of their rape of the lesbian Lorraine is shattering not only because of the female's pain but also because the dazed Lorraine in turn kills the one male who has cared for her as a surrogate father.[11] Lorraine's murder of the kind yet hapless Ben is a textbook case of victim killing victim, but Naylor rejects any suggestion that the marauding males are depraved because they are deprived. Stack argues that economic conditions compromise the identity of the black male. Naylor dismisses such generalities. In a scorching denial of male power she blames the thugs themselves for their inability to exist outside the rat pack:

> They needed the others continually near to verify their existence. When they stood with their black skin, ninth-grade diplomas, and fifty-word vocabularies . . . , those other pairs of tight jeans, suede sneakers, and tinted sunglasses imaged nearby proved that they were alive. And if there was life, there could be dreams of that miracle that would one day propel them into the heaven populated by their gods—Shaft and Superfly. (161)

Talking loudly, scratching their crotches, and calling each other "Man," they feel threatened by any female who ignores what they assume is the power of their sexuality. As one of the males explains in an inadvertent play on gender: "Aw Man, come on. Don't waste your time. . . . She ain't nothing but a woman" (162).

Sociobiologists might agree with his comment in terms of hunting, protecting, and evolution itself, but, like the male novelists of the

1980s, Naylor finds culture more complex than a hierarchy of male prerogative. Her criticism of black men is as extensive as the biodeterminist undervaluing of women. *The Women of Brewster Place* illustrates Nancy Chodorow's position on the primacy of the mother-child bond,[12] Bleier's doubts about the importance of man-the-hunter theories, and Hrdy's evidence about female bonding. Yet Naylor goes further than arguing the equal importance of men and women. Her wilderness is the closed-off world of inner-city tenements, but all males from the rural South to the urban North deserve secondary status in *Brewster Place*. Thus, the epigraph to the novel, Langston Hughes's famous question,

> What happens to a dream deferred?
> Does it dry up
> like a raisin in the sun?

applies only to Naylor's bonded women. Similarly, Hughes's promise of violence in the wake of a dream forever delayed is relevant not to the raping males, who have no dreams beyond Superfly, but, rather, to the women who reaffirm their bond when they tear down the wall during the block party at the end of the novel. *The Women of Brewster Place* was written by a black novelist about black people, but it foregrounds gender, not race.

Naylor's men—always separate, never bonding—are variations of Mattie's girlhood lover, Butch Fuller. Attractive, fun, and unreliable where Mattie is attractive, serious, and determined, Butch personifies the emptiness that Naylor sees at the center of black masculinity: "like puffed air and cotton candy" (14). When he abandons Mattie after getting her pregnant, he acts out the sociological phenomenon of the absent black father. Worse, he does not leave behind what Stack calls a "kinship network." One could argue that Mattie's father is a black man in the home, but when he thrashes his daughter for turning up pregnant Naylor shows that he defines sexual independence in the female as a threat to the traditional power of the male. Mattie's son is no better. He also betrays her, but in this instance Naylor adds the complicating issue of female indulgence of male whim. Needing a man equal to her strength, Mattie spoils the boy rather than rears him: "She had carefully pruned his spirit to rest only in the enclaves of her will, and she had willed so little" (43). One could go on tracing Naylor's characterizations of the attorney, the minister, and old Ben the janitor to show that her conclusions are consistent, despite Stack's thesis to the contrary: the black family bond disintegrates because the men are either violent or missing. As another betrayed woman tells Mattie: "Let's face it, Mattie. All the good men are either dead or waiting to be born" (61).

The Women of Brewster Place, then, reverses the traditional model of American fiction and banishes the male from the female group. For the most part Naylor's women have many of the qualities that sociobiologists attribute to men. They are aggressive and protective, and they bond naturally. When society shuts them out another woman takes them in. Male novelists from Cooper to Dickey illustrate R. W. B. Lewis's notion of the wilderness as the testing ground for the American Adam, but Naylor sees the archetypes of the Madonna and Eve. Her women bring not the threat of sexuality, as Cooper would have it, but, rather, the promise of nurturing. The woman who shelters Mattie and her son, for example, is named Miss Eva, and Naylor clearly identifies her as the source of female bonding. Human society develops from the solidarity of women, for they raise the progeny while the males wander the world alone: "In the unabashed fashion of the old, Miss Eva unfolded her own life and secret exploits to Mattie. . . . The young black woman and the old yellow woman sat in the kitchen for hours, blending their lives so that what lay behind one and ahead of the other became indistinguishable" (34). Where traditional male writers celebrate bonding primarily in the presence of aggression or during a confrontation with the unknown, Naylor suggests an unbroken attachment among women that stretches back to the Garden. Mattie is Naylor's new-world Eve, the inheritor of Miss Eva's wisdom and the dispenser of female strength. Another exploitative man may accuse a pregnant woman of being good for nothing but "babies and bills," but, while holding the woman, Mattie rocks her out of pain and into the bond that Naylor finds uninterrupted for all wronged females from Eve through Clytemnestra to the women of today: "She rocked her over Aegean seas so clean they shone like crystal, so clear the fresh blood of sacrificed babies torn from their mother's arms and given to Neptune could be seen like pink froth on the water. She rocked her on and on, past Dachau, where soul-gutted Jewish mothers swept their children's entrails off laboratory floors. They flew past the spilled brains of Senegalese infants whose mothers had dashed them on the wooden sides of slave ships. And she rocked on" (103). The power of religious ritual traditionally limited to patriarchy—priest, minister, rabbi—is here assigned to Mattie when she washes the young woman clean of her agony and thereby baptizes her into the promise of the female bond.

Bonding among women weakens only in the presence of lesbianism. Naylor deftly suggests the uncertainty that arises when the "homosocial" shades into the homoerotic,[13] and she exposes women who deny one of their own. On the one hand, "the two," as the lesbians are called by the people of Brewster Place, try to live independently of men. They have no interest in the lovers and husbands of the local women. On the other hand, lesbian independence threatens the identity of women who define themselves according to approval by males. The lesbians' "friendly indifference to the men on the street was an insult to the women as a brazen flaunting of unnatural ways" (131). The continuum that Eve Kosofsky Sedgwick finds among female bonds, be they homosocial or homoerotic, does not hold in *The Women of Brewster Place*. For Naylor the issue is not sexuality but, rather, self-sufficiency. The women on the block fear the two because the lesbians do not care for men. Females who are free of the cycle of weak males, violent domestic relationships, and unexpected pregnancy are denied the solace of bonding except among themselves. Lorraine's rape by the strutting adolescents, who are no more than a parody of bonding, is a physical male rendering of an unvoiced female resentment.

The block party at the conclusion of the novel, which reasserts the female bond when the women gather to tear down a wall, hardly compensates for the rejection of the two. But it does illustrate what Naylor calls an "ebony phoenix," always female, always potent, often aggressive. Women bond imperfectly, observes Sarah Hrdy. In *The Women of Brewster Place* Gloria Naylor shows that what matters is that they bond at all.

II

In discussing new patterns in the historical development of American fiction which have not been identified before, I argue that representative contemporary male writers indirectly challenge the format that posits two or more men bonding beyond civilization in order to avoid the inhibiting female. The female inhibits, so traditional male novelists believe, because she represents society, restraint, mortality, and time. In rewriting the paradigm, Busch, Irving, and other recent authors do not deny the enduring lure of the wilderness in contemporary American culture. Like their forerunners, they identify the territory on the far side of the border as a realm of potentially limitless space, as a domain of freedom from constraint, as a promise of immortality. To reject the wilderness would be to dismiss a staple of the American myth, something these writers cannot do, as shown by their many allusions to the traditional novels of the canon. Yet they do question the long-honored stipulation that calls for avoidance of women as defilers of a virgin space. When the bonded males in Busch's novel—or Irving's or Russo's—cross the border, they find either that the woman has already preceded them or that they need to take her along. Rather than threaten the bond, women strengthen it, and they do so in such a persuasive manner that one sees the new American novel signaling different directions for American culture.

A general point about the directions is that they are not exclusive but inclusive. Both genders now enter a territory that was once the private domain of males. Such may not be the case in contemporary novels of female relationships. Female bonding has been inclusive in traditional American fiction. One thinks immediately of *Uncle Tom's Cabin* (1852), but one also concedes that the women in Stowe's masterwork are generally not aggressive. For the most part their bonding is a matter of nurture, and Stowe's women of solidarity stand ready to embrace all who need solace. One notes with interest, then, both the sterility associated with female bonding in Wiggins's *John Dollar* and the violence in Naylor's *The Women of Brewster Place*. In these novels males are either destroyed or repudiated, just as females usually are in traditional American fiction. Thus, one wonders whether a reversed paradigm is now in the offing *and* whether gender politics is the driving force behind the reversal.

There are many significant differences between *John Dollar* and *Brewster Place*, of course, but for my concerns a primary distinction is that Wiggins laments the elimination of the male in the presence of female bonding while Naylor insists on it. Although the former novel takes for its setting a historical moment nearly a century ago and the latter is set on the margins of middle-class society, both are politically sensitive to the general upheaval in gender relationships which has changed most of America since the 1960s. *John Dollar* suggests that institutionalized male authority must be challenged, that nature itself will overthrow King George and his patriarchal representatives. Yet Wiggins also shows that individual males do not necessarily personify patriarchal dominance, that love between female and male is creative, and that aggressive female bonding can spin out of control, eventually cannibalizing reciprocal relationships. Females first devour the male in *John Dollar* and then destroy each other.

Women turn on women in *The Women of Brewster Place* also, but only when the lesbians are deemed deviant by the homosocial females who bond to protect themselves from men. Wiggins regrets the negation of creative bonding between individual women and men during aggressive consolidations of the female bond. Naylor regrets nothing of the sort.

Thus, I conclude this section with a query that points to an irony: Will contemporary novels of female bonding written by women reject the long needed but now realized alteration of the tradition established by canonical American fiction, an alteration that is urgently advocated in contemporary novels of male bonding written by men? Reading Wiggins and Naylor in conjunction with Russo and Woiwode, one wonders whether a new exclusivity regarding gender is to be formalized just at the moment when male authors have finally realized that women belong in the wilderness.

III

These issues have engaged the popular press. An article in *Time* magazine, however ephemeral, will surely reach a larger audience than an exquisitely written contemporary novel such as Joan Chase's *During the Reign of the Queen of Persia* (1983), but mass media often deal in diminished ideas. Nevertheless, one notes with interest that, just before the release of the troubling movie about female bonding, *Thelma & Louise* (1991), *Time* published an essay by Pico Iyer which poses a question to frame what Iyer sees as the current tendency to empower females by bashing males: "As it is, students are being taught in school that 'patriarchal' is the worst kind of insult, and misogynists must be sought out everywhere. But what is the term for misogyny in reverse?"[14] Titling the essay with another question, "Are Men Really So Bad?" Iyer illustrates how sensitive issues irritate popular nerves. His immediate reference is Bret Easton Ellis's *American Psycho* (1991)—a novel in which a male psychopath perpetrates unspeakable horrors on women—but his primary complaint is that Mary Gaitskill's novel *Two Girls, Fat and Thin* (1991) has not been greeted with an outrage similar to that which confronted Ellis even though it denigrates men to the extreme of ridiculousness. The reason, he suggests, is that *Two Girls, Fat and Thin* was written by a woman: "But it is very much to be hoped that the outrage would be no less if Ellis' monster had been a woman, or more of its victims men" (94). Given the absurdities of politically correct prickliness, one finds it difficult to imagine an outcry if the pronouns of the debate were reversed and every woman in a novel or film were treated as the oppressor: "the interaction of the sexes, like everything else, can only be demeaned if it is caricatured as a contest of black against white" (94).

My point is not to glorify an essay as fleeting as Iyer's but to confirm that questions of male or female bonding are not confined to the pages of arcane journals and little read fiction. An insignificant filler for university newspapers called *U: The National College Newspaper,* for example, featured in its issue for March 1991 a front-page article with the following headline: "Feminist Movement May Suffer as Today's Students Shun Label."[15] Written by Dana Di Filippo and Laura E. Wexler, the article notes that many college women equate feminism with females clinching teeth, burning bras, and screaming "Death to white males." More significant, these women define feminism as a suspect political movement designed to deny femininity and thereby to negate identity.

No doubt these university students would agree with the current pressure to decenter masculinity by displacing patriarchy. Yet their enthusiasm would likely be more engaged by the argument that the way to challenge patriarchy is to rewrite the old equation of women and passivity and then to relocate females on the traditional male hunting grounds of action. To understand the radical nature of such a revision of culture one might imagine Cooper's *The Last of the Mohicans* (1826) with Cora alive, with Alice spurning Duncan, and with Cora and Alice striking off into the wilderness on their own. Such a refiguring of the paradigmatic plot of masculine adventure would have been the stuff of fantasy and science fiction until recently, but the female writers I am concerned with do indeed revise the plot. Not one of them is enamored of fantasy.

For a final illustration of how serious gender issues have been oversimplified by the popular press one should recall the atmosphere of show biz which surrounded the release of the movie *Thelma & Louise. Time,* for example, featured the film in a cover story with the catchy title "Gender Bender," but, despite the superficiality of the article, the author Richard Schickel pointed out the paradoxical extremes of reactions to the film.[16] A tale of unexpected adventure and female bonding that turns violent and suicidal, *Thelma & Louise* was greeted as both a celebration of feminism and a betrayal of feminism. Contemporary confusion over the issue of female bonding, especially bonding that appropriates the male narrative of quest for its frame, is revealed in the following paragraph from Schickel's article:

It [*Thelma & Louise*] is, according to Miami *Herald* movie reviewer Bill Cosford, "a butt-kicking feminist manifesto . . . which sweeps you along for the ride." No, says Sheila Benson, a Los Angeles *Times* film critic, it is a betrayal of feminism, which, as she understands it, "has to do with responsibility, equality, sensitivity, understanding—not revenge, retribution or sadistic behavior." (52)

The question is whether such oversimplifications of serious issues as Gaitskill's *Two Girls, Fat and Thin* and Ridley Scott's *Thelma & Louise* take advantage of uncertainty or serve as turning points in the debate. Terrence Rafferty, for instance, describes the film as "crazily over-stuffed Hollywood entertainment," and he argues that the feminist justification that the script "provides for the heroines' behavior doesn't make their actions any less preposterous."[17] The result, says Rafferty, is a movie with all "the hellbent energy of a drive-in exploitation picture" (86).

What *Thelma & Louise* does suggest about female bonding, however, is that an unexpected acquisition of freedom eroticizes as well as empowers. The character Louise may begin the plunge beyond the border by assuming the traditionally male role of adventurer to Thelma's conventional female role of passive retainer, but by the end of the film Thelma is the leader because, the movie dubiously suggests, she has awakened to the proximity of eroticism and violence. If female self-assertion leads to death, as *Thelma & Louise* says it does, then one is back in the world of Kate Chopin's *The Awakening* (1899). The dilemma is whether the complexities of female bonding require separation of the genders. If so, one wonders, then, are serious novels by women in the 1980s no more than a rewriting of the paradigmatic male text from a contemporary female perspective? *Thelma & Louise* makes the mistake of exalting the cultural myth that frustrated women need only good sex with an attractive man to ease their confusion, and thus the film is more male fantasy than female empowerment. The novels of female bonding which I discuss avoid this error, but in doing so they raise a startling question: Does female bonding require not the eroticism of the woman but the elimination of the man?

IV

In general, one understands the tradition of women's novels in America to emphasize the domestic, the sentimental, or the romantic. In these narratives women normally eschew both the bond and the quest. Chopin's *Awakening* is an exemplary fiction that is also a case in point. Vaguely wondering "what she meant by 'life's delirium,'" but suffering its impact nonetheless, Chopin's heroine Edna Pontellier rebuffs a bond with the motherly Adelle Ratignolle and fumbles a bond with the rebellious Mademoiselle Reisz.[18] Worse, Edna recognizes the quest but resists its lure. Hesitating to cross the border between soci-

ety and wilderness, described in *The Awakening* as the beach between
land and sea, she drowns rather than join Ishmael, Huck, or Ed Gentry
in sailing over the water. A century later Ruth and Sylvie in Marilynne
Robinson's *Housekeeping* (1981) will first bond and then negotiate a
danger-fraught bridge across a vast lake to meet the quest that will
make their lives. That the townspeople who remain behind think Ruth
and Sylvie have drowned is an irony that readers of Chopin—or, for
that matter, of Melville, Twain, and Dickey—will not miss.

Before defining specific concerns in the following chapters, let
me name the novels relevant to my discussion: Joan Didion, *A Book
of Common Prayer* (1977); Diane Johnson, *The Shadow Knows* (1974);
Marilynne Robinson, *Housekeeping* (1981); Mona Simpson, *Anywhere but
Here* (1986); Hilma Wolitzer, *Hearts* (1980); Meg Wolitzer, *This Is Your
Life* (1988); Joan Chase, *During the Reign of the Queen of Persia* (1983);
and Lisa Alther, *Other Women* (1984). I also comment on Douglas Ungar's *Leaving the Land* (1984) because a male writer's account of the
contemporary woman's need to bond is relevant. I simplify here what
may be complex later: in women's novels of the 1980s, the females
appropriate the male plot of the quest, but they revise the imperative
to bond. Their bonds do not generally hold. Even more important, at
least when compared to novels by males in the 1980s, men are excluded from the bond.

In the following chapter I examine the question of what it means
to be a heroine in a genre representing a world long defined by men.
Using the conclusions of Rachel M. Brownstein and Carolyn G. Heilbrun, I discuss the status of women in fiction when the closure of
marriage is not the primary issue. My general point here is that contemporary female novelists of bonding between women do not repudiate the patriarchal text but, instead, revise it to accommodate females
who accept the traditional masculine call to the quest and step beyond
society to the wilderness. Chapter 3 focuses primarily on bonding
between mothers and daughters. Nancy Chodorow's conclusions about
the reproduction of mothering are central to debates about female
relationships, but, as one would expect about so explosive a subject,
many scholars dispute her. Thus, I discuss both Chodorow's analysis
and responses to it by Elizabeth Abel, Judith Kegan Gardiner, and
Janice G. Raymond. Such a discussion is pertinent because the affinity
between mothers and daughters shapes fiction by women in the 1980s.

In the remainder of the book I turn to these current novels by
first discussing an interesting variation. The latest feminist movement
in America dates from the 1960s, and thus the novels of the 1970s are
among the first to chart the social changes wrought by the revaluation

of gender. In chapter 4 I read Didion's *A Book of Common Prayer* and Johnson's *The Shadow Knows* as tales that revise the linear plot of the male quest in order to accommodate the new heroine but which do not banish men from women's bonds. Didion and Johnson suggest that one need not repudiate the male when rewriting the canonical narrative. Female novelists of the 1980s generally disagree, as I show in chapter 5 by discussing Robinson's *Housekeeping* as the watershed novel of female bonding in American literature. Highlighting allusions to Melville, Twain, and other male authors of the canon, Robinson nevertheless revises the text by rejecting the man. In doing so she formalizes the gender exclusivity that has been a primary sign of American women's writing in the 1980s. In chapter 6 I focus on female novelists who have followed Robinson both in adapting the American literary paradigm—rather than repudiating it—and in banishing men from female relationships: Mona Simpson, Hilma Wolitzer, Meg Wolitzer, Joan Chase, and Lisa Alther. I am concerned here with such variations as sibling rivalry, mother-daughter bonding, and lesbianism, but I find that my general points about revising the paradigm and rejecting the male are consistent throughout these novels.

The final chapter is not a conclusion but a coda. Rather than summarize what has already been said, I speculate about the issues of female bonding and women in the wilderness when examined from the point of view of a male writer. Douglas Ungar is a contemporary of the female authors discussed here, and I read his *Leaving the Land* as an examination of similar material from a different perspective. In general, Ungar honors the new heroine in the wilderness but finds that she pursues the old narrative of marriage. This is a dilemma not easily resolved. Female novelists of the 1980s have recast a tradition that has shaped American literature for more than two centuries. The irony, however, is that, just when Frederick Busch, John Irving, and Larry Woiwode close the gap between genders which is a staple of the standard American novel, Joan Chase, Lisa Alther, and Marilynne Robinson reopen it. One can only wonder whether gender exclusivity is to be privileged in novels of female bonding while recent novels of male bonding free the wilderness to women.[19]

Notes

1. Donald J. Greiner, *Women Enter the Wilderness: Male Bonding and the American Novel of the 1980s* (Columbia: University of South Carolina Press, 1991).

2. Lionel Tiger and Robin Fox, *The Imperial Animal* (New York: Holt, Rinehart and Winston, 1971).

3. Ruth Bleier, *Science and Gender: A Critique of Biology and Its Theories on Women*

(New York: Pergamon, 1984). Donna J. Haraway, "In the Beginning Was the Word: The Genesis of Biological Theory," *Signs* 6 (Spring 1981): 469–81.

4. Susan K. Harris, "'But is it any *good?*': Evaluating Nineteenth-Century American Women's Fiction," *American Literature* 63 (March 1991): 54.

5. Lionel Tiger, *Men in Groups* (New York: Random House, 1969), 171–72.

6. Sarah Blaffer Hrdy, *The Woman That Never Evolved* (Cambridge, Mass.: Harvard University Press, 1981).

7. Marianne Wiggins, *John Dollar* (New York: Harper and Row, 1989).

8. My information about the title may be found in Richard Gehr, "Sins of the Flesh Eaters: Marianne Wiggins's Carnal Knowledge," *Village Voice*, 21 March 1989, 50.

9. Carol B. Stack, *All Our Kin: Strategies for Survival in a Black Community* (New York: Harper and Row, 1974).

10. Gloria Naylor, *The Women of Brewster Place* (1982; New York: Penguin, 1985).

11. For an analysis of the rape scene, see Laura E. Tanner, "Reading Rape: *Sanctuary* and *The Women of Brewster Place*," *American Literature* 62 (December 1990): 559–82.

12. Nancy Chodorow, *The Reproduction of Mothering: Psychoanalysis and the Sociology of Gender* (1978; Berkeley: University of California Press, 1979).

13. The term *homosocial* is Eve Kosofsky Sedgwick's. See *Between Men; English Literature and Male Homosocial Desire* (New York: Columbia University Press, 1985).

14. Pico Iyer, "Are Men Really So Bad?" *Time* (22 April 1991): 94.

15. Dana Di Filippo and Laura E. Wexler, "Feminist Movement May Suffer as Today's Students Shun Label," *U: The National College Newspaper*, March 1991, 1–2.

16. Richard Schickel, "Gender Bender," *Time* (24 June 1991): 52–56.

17. Terrence Rafferty, "Outlaw Princesses," *New Yorker* (3 June 1991): 86.

18. Kate Chopin, *The Awakening*, ed. Margaret Culley (1899; New York: W. W. Norton, 1976), 56.

19. As a relevant sidelight, one might consider Andrea Dworkin's *Mercy* (New York: Four Walls Eight Windows, 1991) as a novel that recommends the most extreme position possible when repudiating men: killing them. But, as Wendy Steiner writes in the *New York Times Book Review* (15 September 1991), "Ms. Dworkin's argument, proceeding from pain, may be moving, but it is also intolerant, simplistic and often just as brutal as what it protests. . . . Perhaps the most glaring weakness in Ms. Dworkin's esthetic is her indifference to other people's pain. . . . If all women are either victims or collaborators and all men are rapists, can the cry for mercy fall on any but deaf ears?" (11) More to the point are two scholarly studies of the separate spheres of men and women in nineteenth-century America and how these gender spaces changed in the early twentieth century: Ted Ownby, *Subduing Satan: Religion, Recreation, and Manhood in the Rural South, 1865–1920* (Chapel Hill: University of North Carolina Press, 1991); and Paula Baker, *The Moral Frameworks of Public Life: Gender, Politics, and the State of Rural New York, 1870–1930* (New York: Oxford University Press, 1991). Michael S. Kimmel's comment about the two books is relevant:

> The boundaries between women's and men's worlds were both more pervasive and more fluid than we had thought earlier. Their books suggest that many of the historical tensions that characterized the last decades of the nineteenth century and the first decades of the twentieth—the growing division between city and country, church and state, home and work, north/east and south/west, "wet" and "dry," unionized workers and autonomous farmers and artisans—were gendered tensions,

marked by deepening anxieties about women's Christian piety and chaste virtue and men's moral license and economic probity. What's more, when these worlds collided at the turn of the century, Paula Baker and Ted Ownby agree, it was the women's world that triumphed.

See "Music of the Spheres," *Nation* 12, no. 19 (August 1991): 205–8.

Chapter Two

Female Bonding and Literary
Heroines

In traditional American literature the hero reconnoiters new territory while the heroine reclaims old space. The result for the woman
is the security of closure. The reward for the man is the open-end-
edness of quest. In the contemporary novel of female adventure, however, the woman stakes her claim to the wilderness. But, if she is not
Natty Bumppo slaying the Iroquois or Ishmael hunting the whale or
Ike McCaslin tracking the bear, what is she? When, in other words,
does a woman become a heroine?

I am not concerned here with what might be called, from a white
male point of view, "appropriating the Otherness" of women. I am
interested, however, in the complexity of recent American fiction, a
complexity in which female novelists play a major role. In this chapter
I discuss the problematics of women writing heroines in a narrative
tradition defined by men. Rachel M. Brownstein and Carolyn G. Heilbrun provide the theoretical perspective and Mona Simpson's *Anywhere
but Here* the exemplum.

I

In her "Notes" at the conclusion of *Becoming a Heroine: Reading
about Women in Novels* (1982), Rachel M. Brownstein concedes the
difficulty of defining *heroine:* "The term 'heroine' is even harder than
'hero' is; I can make no useful preliminary definition, since its prob-
lematic nature is my subject."[1] She does, however, call attention to
relatively recent efforts to distinguish between the terms *hero* and
heroine by referring to such scholarship as Ellen Moers's term *heroinism*
(*Literary Women*, 1976) and Carolyn Heilbrun's position that women
who have been excluded from traditional definitions of heroism should
look for models among exemplary men, rather than women, in literature (*Reinventing Womanhood*, 1979). Like Brownstein, I am less interested in defining a new model of female heroism than in investigating

the complexities of the term as it is worked out in a number of contemporary fictions. I find Heilbrun's argument persuasive, as I do the following statement from Brownstein: "The ideas of the remarkable individual and the achieved self are presented in novels about women, I think, in such a way as to emphasize the literariness and the limitations of the heroic idea" (299).

As Brownstein points out—following Freud—the female reader's admiration of the beautiful and beloved heroine who graces the romantic novel is primarily an attraction to idealized versions of the self. This is why the standard marriage plot of traditional fiction is largely about the heroine's need to confirm the self, to validate her value by preparing herself in such a way as to be chosen from among all other available women by the man. In such novels male love guarantees female worth. The issue becomes not quest but confirmation: the hero sallies forth to the wilderness, but the heroine stays behind beside the hearth. Her territory is not the theatening adventure but, rather, the predictable routine. Note Brownstein's pointed use of the word *wilderness*: "Her search for perfect love through an incoherent, hostile wilderness of days is the plot that endows the aimless (life) with aim" (xv). One wonders about the irony of a trek through such a territory, of the female's embracing the plot of the Other in order to know the self. Yet this is what the novel has traditionally taught. Women read novels to learn about their lives, then move from the novel into life, confident of the happy ending: "Reader, I married him," as Charlotte Brontë memorably wrote. Commenting on the continued relevance of classic English novels of female fate, Brownstein observes, "The novel about a chaste heroine and her gender-determined destiny raises and ponders such still-pressing questions as to whether intimacy and identity can be achieved at once, and whether they are mutually exclusive, entirely desirable, and, indeed, other than imaginary" (xix). In other words, may the self (read female) embrace the Other (read male) to validate the self in any place except fiction? Does the bonding between female readers and literary heroines free the reader herself to the status of heroine, or does such bonding enclose the reader in the coils of convention? Brownstein is clear: "What the female protagonist of a traditional novel seeks—what the plot moves her toward—is an achieved, finished identity, realized in conclusive union with herself-as-heroine. Her marriage or death at the end of the narrative signifies this union" (xxi).

The novels that concern me are not conventional and surely are not illustrations of classic formulas. The goal in *Anywhere but Here* and *During the Reign of the Queen of Persia* is not to embrace Other to confirm self but to bond with another version of the self in order to exclude Other. This goal is not always achieved. As Brownstein writes, "It is traditional for women in fiction to be aware of images of women, and of their power" (xxiv). To illustrate she cites Chaucer's Wife of Bath as a heroine very much aware that women in literature can greatly influence readers. Yet there is danger in a reader's inclination to assess women in literary terms, to believe that female readers can be fictional heroines, as novels as venerable as Jane Austen's *Northanger Abbey* (1818) and Henry James's *The Turn of the Screw* (1898) have shown. The point in many contemporary novels of female bonding is not to idealize the threatened yet honorable woman but, instead, to confront contradictions that are apparently unavoidable when heroines insist on determining individual value according to gender. Brownstein's shrewd description of traditional novels does not always apply to recent fiction about women: "The implicit message of the heroine-centered novel is double: the novel proposes a sophisticated version of the ideal of romance as the heroine comes to transcendent closure, but that ideal is undercut as transcendence and closure are characterized as romantic, as proper to Art, not Life" (xxvi).

Unlike canonical male writers of the American paradigm, these female novelists—Mona Simpson, Joan Chase, Hilma Wolitzer—insist on an ironic use of such traditional fictional staples as the wilderness and of such conventional literary characters as the heroine. The need to marry in order to determine self is not the issue in *Hearts* or *House-keeping,* just as neither Hilma Wolitzer nor Marilyn Robinson ever asks, with Trollope, "can you forgive her?" when the heroine lingers over questions of whom to marry and why.[2] Validating traditional notions of femininity is never the primary goal of such characters as Robinson's Ruth and Simpson's Ann.

Brownstein rightly argues that "novelists agree that from a man's petition that she marry him a woman learns to know herself" (14), but she would also likely concede that such is not always the case in recent novels of female bonding. As Brownstein reveals about her own experience, "Domestic life is dull and disorderly" (25). Why not, then, the writers I am interested in ask, light out for the territory? Instead of Mrs. Gaskell, why not write as Mark Twain? My point is that, rather than refashion the traditional domestic novel to accommodate contemporary social trends, these writers appropriate the paradigmatic tale of bonding and the ensuing quest. The result is the canonical (male) American novel written from a female perspective. Huck Finn may occasionally dress as a girl to slip out of a tight spot, but he would never welcome Becky Thatcher on the raft. The raft, like the ocean and the forest, is the clubhouse for the league of gentlemen. In the American novel of male bonding women are out of place once the bonded males cross the border to pursue an adventure in the territory. Mona Simpson, Hilma Wolitzer, and Joan Chase shatter the sanctity of this "venerable tradition" by first substituting females for males, then denying the adventure to the men who once thought it their own. In doing so, these female writers ponder the long-established equation between fictional heroines and interiority, between females and the received notion that novels about women should reflect a woman's inner life. In other words, the authors of *Anywhere but Here* and *During the Reign of the Queen of Persia* subvert the convention described by Brownstein as the standard relationship between female readers and novels by women: "In life as in novels, women read romances, and look up from the pages with their vision blurred. Real women, like realistic novels, are haunted by the shaping shadow of romance" (32).

Brownstein understands that the feminist woman resists capitulation to the paradox that urges females simultaneously to long for perfection and to concede inadequacy. Novels by women often encourage such a dilemma, however inadvertently; one thinks of Chopin's *Awakening* and Edith Wharton's *House of Mirth* (1905). Yet Brownstein also argues that the need for female readers to see themselves as heroines is a difficult tendency to counter. This is because many novels by women traditionally indulge the reader's desire to shape her own life according to moral qualities defined by literature. It is as if Don Quixote rode into Jane Austen's *Emma* (1816), read the novel, then hurried out to find a wife. "English novels," says Brownstein, "imply the fiction that only one husband can ever be chosen" (146). Contemporary American female novelists reject this plot.

II

Although Carolyn Heilbrun, unlike Brownstein, is not specifically interested in fiction, her analysis of the conflict between the general anonymity of women and the need to tell their stories is an acute and relevant point of departure for a study of bonding in contemporary novels by women.[3] Her observation, for example, that women "who acquire power are more likely to be criticized for it than are the men who have always had it" (16) addresses the dilemma Adele faces in *Anywhere but Here*. The absence of power directly affects literature, for it results in a lack of narrative for those who wish to write their own lives. Narrative *is* power, as women novelists in the 1980s know. Yet the articulation of story is often silenced by the domesticity of space.

The point is that access to a territory traditionally reserved for males means a different narrative for women told in a new voice.

Thus, one conclusion I will amplify in the following chapters is that contemporary female novelists of bonding between women do not repudiate the patriarchal text but rewrite it. They refuse to let domesticity define them, as the women in, say, Harriet Beecher Stowe's *Uncle Tom's Cabin* do; nor do they die, as do Susanna Rowson's Charlotte (*Charlotte: A Tale of Truth* [1791]) or Chopin's Edna *(The Awakening)*, when they dare to seize the masculine prerogative and step beyond the border between the parlor and the woods. The safety of closure has traditionally been reserved as the goal of female experience, and therefore one is not surprised that the complexities of marriage determine the simplicities of plot in conventional novels by women. But what happens to narrative when the closure of marriage is not a primary issue? What happens when, in Heilbrun's words, female writers show that closure "forbid[s] life to be experienced directly" (20)?

A direct engagement with experience means a conscious plunging into life. It means not killing off Cora Munro and sending Alice back to the settlement but watching them walk the dark forest with Natty Bumppo and his Mohican friends instead. It means not staying on the shore to hear about Moby Dick but sailing on the *Pequod* to find him. These revised narratives sound ridiculous only because traditional American literature requires bonded males to embark on a quest by leaving women behind. Significant alterations in the paradigm have already occurred in novels of male bonding. My argument is that changes have redirected women's fiction as well. Heilbrun correctly observes: "The expression of anger has always been a terrible hurdle in women's personal progress. Above all, the public and private lives cannot be linked, as in male narratives" (25). The public sphere in the novels I discuss is defined as life beyond the home, the life that one identifies with Natty's forest or Ishmael's ocean or Huck's river— the life, in short, that is a metaphor of the wilderness. Although direct expression of anger is not a primary concern in *Anywhere but Here* or *During the Reign of the Queen of Persia*, one understands that in writing women's lives these authors have revised narrative to redirect anger.

Such revision is significant in light of Heilbrun's general thesis that women's silence negates women's story. The absence of a script to follow—other than domesticity or death—means a lack of examples to emulate. One lives one's life through texts. As Heilbrun explains: "What matters is that lives do not serve as models; only stories do that. And it is a hard thing to make up stories to live by. We can only retell and live by the stories we have read or heard" (37). Faced with the expectation of writing the marriage plot and thus acquiescing to the safety of closure, women writers traditionally have found that silence is solace: "anonymity eases women's pains, alleviates the anxiety about the appropriateness of gender" (40). This is not the case in the new novel of female bonding. Simpson's Adele, for instance, is not anonymous and surely not silent. Her daughter Ann is her bonded companion as they break from the kitchen to the territory further west, and one learns that Ann will revise Adele's script by retelling it.[4] Simpson's point is that Ann will grow by having Adele's narrative to read beyond.

I agree with Heilburn that the dilemma confronting the woman who would tell her tale is not so much the restriction of language but the absence of text. But, unlike Heilbrun, I also argue that, while such a quandary is relevant to the American literary tradition, it has lost much of its power to constrain in novels written by women since 1980. These authors not only celebrate female characters bonding but they themselves bond, as it were, with each other as they rewrite the American tale. Referring to Hawthorne's *Scarlet Letter* (1850) and Cather's *O Pioneers!* (1913), Heilbrun writes:

> In both of these novels the woman had lived through her special destiny but left no path behind her for future women, had lived with no community of women, *no sense of bonding with other women*. Not only had these women no stories other than their refusal of the plot in which most women lived, and no women with whom to talk of what they had themselves learned, but they would have been hard put to answer the inevitable question asked of unhappy women: What do you want? (43; my emphasis)

Is a complete life possible, in other words, for the woman who quests beyond society—which she equates with patriarchal control? Surely such possibility is the case in canonical stories of the male quest. Nick Adams at Big Two-Hearted River, Ike McCaslin in the bear-haunted woods, Eugene Henderson in unforgiving Africa—all have ventured beyond society to validate the self. An irony informs this contrast, however, and it is crucial: Nick, Ike, Eugene, and the authors who created them equate civilization with not patriarchal but matriarchal control. Wives, mothers, and Aunt Sallys must be escaped from if the adventure in the wilderness is to be engaged. The issue may be, then, not so much patriarchy versus matriarchy but, rather, the long tradition of American narrative which stipulates death (Cora Munro) or denial (Hester Prynne) to those females who would bond with another companion and walk forcefully into the woods. Women novelists since 1980 have rewritten the text of that tradition.

To do so they have bonded with one another by speaking to one another through narrative. Heilbrun quotes Deborah Cameron in a statement that I find relevant to the novel after 1980: "Men do not control meaning at all. Rather women *elect* to use modes of expression men can understand because that is the best way of getting men to listen" (43). The issue may indeed be power, but the larger point here is that recent women novelists have revised rather than rejected the classic American text of first the bond then the adventure. The impulse to retell the tale is the impulse to power. It is also a repudiation of the guilt that Heilbrun describes as engulfing women who are isolated in nuclear families, "each supposing herself a monster when she did not fit the acceptable narrative of a female life" (45). The heroines of Mona Simpson, Joan Chase, and Hilma Wolitzer sense but refuse the lure of that guilt. Heilbrun argues that narratives of female lives will be possible only at the moment when women no longer live in stories determined by men. My point is that this moment is already here.

The crux is the quest. If writing a woman's life has traditionally meant the plot of either marriage or eroticism—and it has—then the adventure in the wilderness has been strictly defined as the domain of men. Ulysses sails for glory. Penelope stays home. Or, more to the point, Robert Lebrun leaves for Mexico. Edna Pontellier drowns. It may well be, as Erik Erikson affirms, that crises pivotal enough to reverse life patterns often occur at an earlier age for males than for females, but such distinctions do not explain why one rarely equates women's narrative with lighting out for the territory. One of Heilbrun's concerns is the scarcity of female treks beyond the border: "For women who wish to live a quest plot, as men's stories allow, indeed encourage, them to do, some event must be invented to transform their lives, all unconsciously, apparently 'accidentally,' from a conventional to an eccentric story" (48). Heilbrun has in mind not a particular novel but a specific life, for she cites the text of George Eliot's adventure when Eliot rejected the claims of the Victorian matron for the status of the fallen woman. Unlike Heilbrun, however, I find that the quest is a staple of new women's fiction, not an eccentricity. *Anywhere but Here* is a case in point. When Adele and her bonded daughter Ann abandon friends, family, and home in order to head west, they follow a trail struck by Leatherstocking and Chingachgook, but they define it in their own terms. Significantly, Simpson does not romanticize the quest. It is not that Adele and Ann die or are forced to turn back toward domesticity, as they would surely have to do were Cooper their author and Natty their guide, but, rather, that their quest does not necessarily bring closure or success. Adele exemplifies the courage and imagination, for instance, to see the race through to its end. Unlike her sister, who defines the female self according to woman's safety, Adele tries to rewrite the narrative of marriage, kitchen, and nursery. But Simpson shows that to escape in space is not to escape in time.

In making this point, she rewrites, from a perspective of woman's narrative, a thesis first argued by R. W. B. Lewis in *The American Adam* (1955).[5] Using Natty Bumppo as his illustration of the literary hero perpetually on the quest, Lewis stressed that, although Natty can get away in space—that is, in distance—from western New York state and its encroaching settlers, he cannot avoid time's inevitable specter of aging. Natty completes his quest in the far reaches of the West, but by the time he does so he is an old, old man. True to novels of female bonding in the 1980s, Simpson revises this long-lived paradigm. Time for Adele means not a clock but an era. Age is always a factor, of course, but the larger concern is that Adele is already a mother when she begins the quest and, thus, has been raised in a time before lighting out for the territory was an option for a female parent. Allowing Adele to get away to California, Simpson shows, nevertheless, that Adele cannot complete the rewriting of the standard woman's plot of courtship and marriage because she has been shaped in a different time. Ann, however, is another matter. Raised after the first successes of the feminist movement—that is, after about 1970—Ann at first naturally models her narrative on her mother's story but only, finally, to reject it. Simpson's tale counters Heilbrun's concern: "For the young woman, . . . for whom the female destiny of flirtation, wedding, and motherhood is insufficient or even unattractive, youth is less a time of hope than a time of uncertainty, at worst a time of depression" (51). Ann breaks free of the conventional woman's text because, while completing the quest, she watches Adele. She understands intuitively what her mother cannot accept: that a woman's identity is no longer defined by a man's pleasure. Her destiny is thus not blunted, as is Edna Pontellier's or Lily Bart's, but, instead, open-ended, as is Natty Bumppo's and Nick Adams's.

The changes I am arguing have taken place in American women's fiction primarily in the last fifteen years. Unlike some commentators (including Heilbrun), I do not believe that black authors have been the principal rewriters of women's lives. Gloria Naylor, Toni Morrison, and Alice Walker are of the first importance, but so are Joan Chase, Mona Simpson, and Marilynne Robinson. It may be true, as Morrison remarks, that black women write differently from white women, but the force for revising the female text is an issue of gender, not of race.

One may even suggest (as I do in *Women Enter the Wilderness*) that gender itself is not always the deciding factor, that cultural imperatives have precipitated a revaluation of the role of women in contemporary novels by males who are sensitive enough to intuit the changes— Frederick Busch, John Irving, and Larry Woiwode among them. The issue is not to point blame or to distribute praise but, rather, to show how recent variations of the female quest encourage women to find bonded companions in other women who are not historical figures, absent, or dead. The interesting question, which I discuss in the following chapters, is whether the newly found bonds are maintained with the fervor one expects of Natty-Chingachgook and Huck-Jim.

One answer may involve the institution of marriage as it is acted out in late twentieth-century life and the fiction that reflects it. Insisting that "marriage is the most persistent myth imprisoning women," Heilbrun cites demographic evidence to suggest that since 1970 young women have not married as readily as their mothers (77). The problem for the contemporary novel of female quest is that lovers are not husbands. Once they become husbands the closure defined as marriage subverts the woman's plunge beyond the confines of the social contract. Many observers, feminist and nonfeminist alike, have remarked that the urge to find a husband and lover in one man dooms the woman who would try to achieve such a goal. In *Anywhere but Here* Adele and her sister, Carol, act out the threats to female bonding posed by standard notions of marriage. On the one hand, Adele drives west with the illusion that, by abandoning her husband, she can find a lover who will then become both a husband to her and a father to Ann. On the other hand, Carol elects to stick out her marriage, becomes powerless, and then sides with patriarchal authority in criticizing Adele for embarking on a quest to write her life outside the marriage plot.

How can a woman bond if both narrative and culture insist that her principal tie must be with a husband? This problem is central in contemporary novels of female relationships, but it is a dilemma yet to be totally solved. Heilbrun's summation is relevant:

> Yet, when all the dangers of matrimony have been perceived, there are women who choose to marry, know what they are doing, and decide that life with a man, with or without children, is what they desire. With rights now to their own property and earnings, with rights to their children, with rights to make contracts and to function as autonomous individuals in the world, they still choose to join with a man. It is for these women, and for the men who choose to love them and to stay with them, that

new definitions and a new reality about marriage must be not only lived but narrated. (89)

Literary evidence suggests that a new marriage plot is only partially written in the contemporary novel of female bonding. In *Anywhere but Here* the husband is left behind once the woman initiates the quest. In Hilma Wolitzer's *Hearts* the husband dies after six weeks of marriage. In Meg Wolitzer's *This Is Your Life* the husband is not a factor. In Joan Chase's *During the Reign of the Queen of Persia* the various husbands are utterly insignificant. In Lisa Alther's *Other Women* the husbands have been divorced. The single result of these multiple variations is that the old marriage plot still lingers, but with a notable exception, an exception not available to Charlotte Temple, Cora Munro, Hester Prynne, Isabel Archer, Edna Pontellier, Maggie Verver, Lily Bart, Nicole Warren, or, for that matter, Scarlett O'Hara: the wives turn to other women for the bond.

Heilbrun observes that friendship between women is not a common narrative in literature and history: "If the friendships of women are considered at all, and that is rare enough, they intrude into the male account the way a token woman is reluctantly included in a male community" (99). The novels I discuss alter the pattern and in doing so break the silence that has been imposed on tales of female bonding. Bonding between women in contemporary fiction may be emotionally intimate and sexually free, and thus the issue is no longer whether women's texts may accommodate bonding but, instead, whether males may be included in the bond. To bond and then quest is to move through the private domain of domesticity to the public sphere of the world. Busch, Irving, and Woiwode illustrate that the male narrative is being revised as energetically as the female's, and their primary means of rewriting the text is to welcome women to relationships that have previously been the stamping grounds of men. One cannot imagine Huck and Jim inviting Becky Thatcher to fish the Mississippi or Jake Barnes and Bill Gorton taking Lady Brett to the Irati River. But recent male writers issue the invitation, as illustrated by Irving, who pointedly names the heroine of *A Prayer for Owen Meany* Hester.

Literary evidence indicates an interesting phenomenon: while the new female writers revise the old story of the quest, they nevertheless subvert the thematic innovation written into the text by their contemporary male peers when they keep the opposite sex from entering the bond. This unexpected irony suggests that the primary quest for the new heroines involves not slaying dragons but escaping gender—that is, sloughing off the conventions of gender which a culture defined by males always already assumes. Thus, wilderness women reform the American narrative to show females assuming the male role of the hero in the male plot of the quest, but in appropriating the text they repudiate the males who have lived it. As Heilbrun notes, "Women laugh together only in freedom, in the recognition of independence and female bonding" (129) The adventure of the quest begins when the illusion of closure ends.

Heilbrun specifically addresses the problem of the female adventure plot in her essay "What Was Penelope Unweaving?" which she collected in *Hamlet's Mother and Other Women* (1990).[6] Arguing that Penelope lives in literary history without a story because she, like all women, is restricted to a marriage tale originally scripted by men, Heilbrun knows that, by contrast, the quest narrative opens up life for the males who would seize it. The challenge is to rewrite gender by retelling the story. Citing the source of patriarchal power as its embodiment in "unquestioned narratives," Heilbrun defines the problem that all women must pose as "how to be freed from the marriage plot and initiated into the quest plot": "How many women today find a script, a narrative, a story to live by?" (*Hamlet's Mother*, 127). The difficulty is not to invent new narratives but, instead, to alter old tales: "Since the male plots, unchanged, will not do for women, and since there are so few female plots, how are we to make the new fictions that will sustain us? Can we combine the female erotic plot and the male quest plot, evolving for ourselves a new tale of female achievement?" (129). Heilbrun hopes that female poets will take the lead in answering the question, but female novelists have already done so.

Anywhere but Here illustrates this seismic change in American literature. With Adele, Simpson personifies the dilemma facing women in the contemporary novel. Stepping into the masculine story of adventure, Adele has been shaped by the feminine story of love. She inadvertently limits her achievement in the public sphere, long understood according to masculine prescriptions, to her attractiveness to men. She marches through the quest while fixing her hair, as it were, and, though she is strong enough to walk away from a home that constrains her in terms of male definitions, she nevertheless suspects subconsciously that emancipation masculinizes her. Part of her quest is to escape the boredom of traditional notions of femaleness, which she attempts through her unconventional ways of fixing meals, but she cannot quite complete revising the story. Final revisions will be the business of her daughter Ann.

Anywhere but Here speaks indirectly to questions raised by Nancy Chodorow about whether mother-daughter relationships are the central feature in female bonding,[7] issues that I will discuss later. For the moment I point to Simpson's novel as one of several fictions of women's bonding that investigate a topic Heilbrun fears has yet to be probed: "I still think that the relation between mothers and daughters is the least explored and understood among all human relationships, and that until we understand it we will not understand something profound about women and female sexuality." (*Hamlet's Mother*, 118). But this very issue dominates the new novel of female bonding, as *Anywhere but Here*—not to mention *During the Reign of the Queen of Persia*, *Hearts*, and *This Is Your Life*—shows. I do not suggest, however, that the relationship between mother and daughter remains as firm as the bond between Natty and Chingachgook. Adele's daughter Ann both joins the quest and understands her mother's role of validating the female by proximity to the male, but in the end she rejects the woman's plot. Ann will not "go to hell" for Adele. In the world of *Anywhere but Here* the bond does not hold.

Notes

1. Rachel M. Brownstein, *Becoming a Heroine: Reading About Women in Novels* (New York: Viking, 1982), 298.

2. Anthony Trollope, *Can You Forgive Her?* (London: Smith, Elder, 1864).

3. Carolyn G. Heilbrun, *Writing a Woman's Life* (1988; New York: Ballantine, 1989).

4. Mona Simpson, *Anywhere but Here* (1986; New York: Vintage, 1988).

5. R. W. B. Lewis, *The American Adam: Innocence, Tragedy, and Tradition in the Nineteenth Century* (1955; Chicago: University of Chicago Press, 1964).

6. Carolyn G. Heilbrun, *Hamlet's Mother and Other Women* (1990; New York: Ballantine, 1991).

7. Nancy Chodorow, *The Reproduction of Mothering: Psychoanalysis and the Sociology of Gender* (1978; Berkeley: University of California Press, 1979).

Chapter Three

Female Bonding and the Identities of Mothers and Daughters

The pivotal moment in female bonding may be the birth of a daughter. Some clinical theorists conclude that mothers bond more forcefully with daughters than with sons because, as they see it, the Oedipus complex requires a boy to break with his mother if he is successfully to grow into his masculine identity. Carolyn Heilbrun observes that mother-daughter relations have not been adequately studied by literary critics, but such is not the case within the discipline of psychoanalysis. The central scholar in this area is Nancy Chodorow, whose findings, though persuasive, are disputed. Discussion of the pros and cons of Chodorow's theory of mothering will establish a frame for an analysis of relationships between mothers and daughters in the new women's fiction.

I

Chodorow's challenge to Freud's theories of gender formation and bonding is one of the most respected feminist accounts of a primary relation, the mother-daughter bond.[1] Psychoanalytical and sociological in nature, much of Chodorow's sophisticated discussion is tangential to this study, but an overview of matters relevant to my interests suggests the complexity of the bonding process. At the risk of coining an oxymoron, one might describe Chodorow as a feminist Freudian. Her general question is why, in most cultures, women rather than men are the principal nurturers of children. In offering various answers, she discusses both the anthropological thesis that societal role training adjusts females to maternal imperatives and the biological position that women naturally inherit the maternal instinct. Chodorow argues, on the contrary, that the bond between mother and daughter is different, albeit unconsciously so, from the bond between mother and son. In other words, the biological mandate for reproduction of the species is always distinct from the social need of mothering. As Chodorow bluntly observes, "women's mothering is one of the few universal and enduring elements of the sexual division of labor" (3). No matter that the late twentieth-century American woman has fewer children than her grandmother; no matter that she often leaves the house in the morning and returns from work at night—the point is that when she goes home in the evening she still faces the primary responsibility for the offspring.

Chodorow believes that psychological theory provides a clear understanding of what she calls "the reproduction of mothering." For my purposes the following observation is pertinent to the study of female bonding in fiction: "women's mothering reproduces itself cyclically. Women, as mothers, produce daughters with mothering capacities and the desire to mother. These capacities and needs are built into and grow out of the mother-daughter relationship itself" (7). Sons are raised differently, and, thus, what Chodorow calls "a division of psychological capacities" leads daughters to reprise the sexual and familial division of labor known as mothering. In short, the mother-daughter affinity—a primary element of female bonding—always reproduces itself.

The Oedipus complex is a distinctive factor here. In her chapter "Gender Differences in the Preoedipal Period" Chodorow insists that female bonding is more inclusive than male bonding because "relational capacities that are curtailed in boys as a result of the masculine oedipus complex are sustained in girls" (93). The effect of this differentiation in the social organization of gender is that the experience of being mothered prepares female children to regard themselves as less separate than their male siblings. Nurtured to develop "more permeable ego boundaries," girls learn early to define themselves according to their relationships with others (93). As Chodorow shows, referring to Freud and Ruth Mack Brunswick, girls retain a preoedipal attachment to the mother for a much longer time than do boys. The reason is that mothers were once daughters and, thus, treat girls differently: "The different length and quality of the preoedipal period in boys and girls are rooted in women's mothering, specifically in the fact that a mother is of the same gender as her daughter and of a different gender from her son. This leads to her experiencing and treating them differently." Such distinctions are not biologically oriented: "Being a grown woman and mother also means having been the daughter of a mother, which affects the nature of her motherliness and the quality of her mothering" (98).

Citing case histories from clinical analysis, Chodorow illustrates that a pattern of "fusion, projection, narcissistic extension, and denial of separateness" is more notable in the early stages of mother-daughter bonding than in mother-son relationships (103). If the mother resists the identity of the daughter as a separate person, then the daughter may later have difficulty defining herself as more than an extension of the mother. What all this means—and it is an irony in the context of the current terminology of literary criticism—is that the male, *not* the female, becomes Other. The Oedipus complex facilitates the stretching of the bond between mother and son at an early age. For women, however, bonding has different, and difficult to resolve, complexities. The issue is not merely that girls long to be like their mothers or even to identify with them. Rather, the daughter and the mother "maintain elements of their primary relationship which means they will feel alike in fundamental ways" (110).

The straining of this bond in contemporary novels by women is both an unexpected phenomenon and a primary cause of the social change that these novels document. In canonical American novels of male bonding an insistent goal of the men who dare to cross into the wilderness is to maintain the bond at all costs. Individual safety and, by extension, the protection of society depend on the enduring relationship of Leatherstocking-Chingachgook and of Ed Gentry–Lewis Medlock. Even in contemporary novels of male bonding—such as Busch's *Sometimes I Live in the Country* and Russo's *The Risk Pool,* novels in which the bonded men both welcome and need the women as they leave society for the territory—the males honor the priority of the bond. Such is not the case, however, in Lisa Alther's *Other Women,* Mona Simpson's *Anywhere but Here,* or Meg Wolitzer's *This Is Your Life.* In these contemporary novels of female bonding the male is excluded, and the bond itself is fragile. One wonders, then, whether literary evidence is at odds with psychoanalytic theory.

Chodorow's account of clinical psychoanalysis finds that girls have a more difficult time during adolescence because of the primacy of the female bond. Mona Simpson, Hilma Wolitzer, Meg Wolitzer, and Joan Chase confront the issue of female bonding as a complication of adolescence, but their conclusions often differ from Chodorow's. Because, argues Chodorow, a girl's transition from the Oedipus complex is more prolonged than a boy's, a female normally is likely to be strongly entangled in familial relationships and, thus, finds the "nonfamilial external world" a more trying experience (134). This is because separation from the mother constitutes a primary task for the female. Yet, as Chodorow points out by citing the clinical observations of Alice Balint and Helene Deutsch, the female desire both to keep daughters bonded to mothers and to send them into the world fosters such an ambivalence that the mother and daughter equate breaking the bond with disaster (135).

One of Chodorow's conclusions illustrates the enormous difference between male and female bonding in fiction. The former often involves learning how to be a man. Ike McCaslin's ritualized initiation by means of the deer and the bear in *Go Down, Moses* and Ed Gentry's struggle to live up to the masculine imperatives of action and strength set by Lewis Medlock in *Deliverance* are classic accounts of what a man must endure to be admitted to the male bond. Such is not the case with female bonding: "A girl is not trying to figure out how to be feminine, but how not to be her mother. Gender-*role* identification is not so involved, whereas it is *the* central issue in the masculine case" (137). Daughters often perceive the feminine role as less desirable because it is less powerful than the masculine role. Bonding for the female is, thus, a paradoxical double: the simultaneous need to guarantee the tie and to sever it forever. Chodorow believes that the severance is never final. Contemporary women writers are not so sure.

Once females achieve adulthood they confront problems generated by the very family structure that nurtured them as children, a structure defined by the combination of woman's mothering and man's dominance. Chodorow understands the dilemma as a matter of relational needs: a female's adult relationship with a male is unlikely to provide total satisfaction because the female experience of having been mothered produces expectations that a male cannot be expected to meet. Thus, while women "are likely to become and remain erotically heterosexual," they are prompted by their own "relational history" to seek emotional gratification beyond erotic attraction to men (200). This is where many contemporary female novelists take issue, however indirectly, with Chodorow's observations. Where Lisa Alther and Mona Simpson show relational ties among women to be tenuous at best and likely to be dissolved at worst, Chodorow argues that females foster significant personal relations with other women in order to reproduce mothering. One basis for her argument is that the female model of bonding features flexible networks rather than an affinity strictly between two individuals, which is the foundation of the male notion of bonding. Despite literary evidence to the contrary, despite such standard accounts of rock-solid male bonding as *The Last of the Mohicans* and *Huckleberry Finn*—not to mention Russo's *Risk Pool* and Woiwode's *Born Brothers*—Chodorow states that in the complex matter of female bonding "women tend to have closer personal ties with each other than men have, and to spend more time in the company of women than they do with men. In our society, there is some sociological evidence that women's friendships are affectively richer than men's" (200). I do not want to prolong a debate about which gender enjoys the "richer" fruits of bonding, but I concede that the qualification indicated by the word *some* in the previous sentence gives pause. Sociological research may indeed suggest that females gather together more often than males, and in different ways, but canonical literature illustrates that the most enduring bonds are between males. Since males have traditionally shaped narrative, they have also controlled content. The new women's novels trace how the female bond generally is in danger of unraveling, though the final break does not always occur. This does not mean that the bonding is negative but, rather, that it is problematical.

Although Chodorow persuasively shows how social relationships among women create the mother-daughter bond that forms females from the preoedipal stage through maturation, she also notes that "deep affective relationships to women are hard to come by on a routine, daily, ongoing basis for many women" (200). The relative isolation of the nuclear family away from multiple friendships and extended kin means that primary relationships other than with one's spouse are today less numerous for women than in the preindustrial age. Sisters, aunts, grandmothers, and best friends are not so readily available. This is why the child is significant. In producing children the woman reproduces mothering and, thus, recreates the one bond that will likely sustain her: "In mothering, a woman acts also on her personal identification with a mother who parents and her own training for women's role" (202). The mother-child bond may be so intense as to make it exclusive on the level of what Chodorow calls "intrapsychic structure" and thereby render a woman's bond to a man superfluous (202). This phenomenon—which Freud recognized (see his essay "On Narcissism")—is significant in literary terms when applied to such novels as Marilynne Robinson's *Housekeeping*. In that splendid novel of female bonding and male insignificance Sylvie rejects the normal socialization of her status as an attractive married woman in her mid-thirties to redirect all her need for bonding to her surrogate daughter, Ruth. Unconcerned with her husband's whereabouts, uninterested in sex, Sylvie illustrates what Helene Deutsch observed clinically as the female who establishes a binary opposition of sexuality and mothering and then chooses the latter (203).[2]

Two general observations are pertinent (recall that Chodorow made them in 1978.) First, mothering in Chodorow's terms is a double process by which a woman maintains her identity as both mother and child. In having offspring the female resolidifies the bond with her own mother. Second, as the male is progressively more absent because of the demands of the workplace and as the primacy of the nuclear family reduces opportunities for bonding with other women, a female's need for such relationships as mothering becomes more acute. Marilynne Robinson, Lisa Alther, and Hilma Wolitzer know these truths.

As a relevant sidelight to Chodorow's discussion and to the revision of the female plot which I am arguing, one should examine *Reinventing Home: Six Working Women Look at Their Home Lives* (1991).[3] This unusual book, written by women whose primary work is in the home, posits that "a rich domestic life is worth having" (1). Aware that "things are not quite right at home," the authors understand that revised notions of female bonding initiated by feminism have necessitated a balance for women who wish to honor traditions of domesticity while simultaneously redefining the relationship between women and home (3). Not all bonded females, in other words, discard the apron to engage the quest. If they do cross the border toward the wilderness, they take the apron with them because they believe that the domestic and the territory can be combined to create what they describe as "a complete life" (4).

Significantly, many of their conclusions support Chodorow's analysis of the mother-daughter bond. In "Full-Time Mother," for example, Mary Beth Danielson discusses the "limbo of full-time parenting," yet insists that "parenting is one of the most spiritual tasks we attempt in our lives" (31). The reason, writes Danielson in an indirect affirmation of Chodorow, is that being a parent requires mothers to recall life as daughters. The mother-daughter relationship, the central factor in Chodorow's account of bonding, always reinvents itself. As Danielson observes, in words that go beyond the specific domesticity of her example, "When I hug my kids and tell them I love them, the little girl in me gets hugged, too" (32).

II

All is not sympathetic mothers bonded to grateful daughters, however. As one suspects, Chodorow's observations are not universally acclaimed. Janice G. Raymond, for example, questions the conclusions when she states her position that female friendship is both personal and political.[4] The point of contention is Chodorow's assumption that "most women are heterosexual," a point that indirectly calls attention to the always lingering politics of lesbianism in discussions of female bonding. Raymond's quarrel with Chodorow is clear and definite because, in general, Raymond rejects Chodorow's belief that women

make a "resolution" in favor of heterosexual bonding. She argues instead that many women are "coerced" into such agreements. Raymond
goes so far as to accuse Chodorow of disrupting analyses of female
bonding to the extent that Chodorow's work does little more than
"bolster and maintain flagging hetero-relations and failed fathers" (52).
Stressing the "importance of women's affection for each other as primary and paradigmatic," Raymond militantly conflates the issues of
female bonding and lesbian politics. Her thesis is unequivocal: "Until
women 'mother' to love and care for other women, the system of
women hetero-reality will not be transformed" (53). To urge men,
observes Raymond, to be more sensitive and caring is to support what
she disparagingly dismisses as a more "touching" version of male bonding, the kind of manliness popularized in such tearjerkers as the movie
Kramer vs. Kramer (54). To celebrate the emergence of newly sensitive
males is to subordinate female friendship to male power.

Reading this rebuttal of Chodorow, one is not surprised that the
primary target of Raymond's angry analysis is patriarchal society. From
her perspective culture conditions women to deny friendship with
women: "This lack of Self-love is grafted onto the female self under
patriarchy. If the graft takes, women who do not love their Selves
cannot love others like their Selves" (4). Raymond finds that female
bonding is nothing less than "an original and primary attraction of
women for women" (5). Rather than *Kramer vs. Kramer*, one is thrust
into the world of *Thelma & Louise*.

Raymond coins the term *Gyn/affection* to define her understanding
of female bonding beyond Chodorow's insights into relationships fos-
tered by mothering: "Gyn/affection is not only a loving relationship
between two or more women; it is also a freely chosen bond which,
when chosen, involves certain reciprocal assurances based on honor,
loyalty, and affection" (9). This account of female bonding articulates
a rationale for excluding males from the bonding process at the same
time that many contemporary male novelists have revised the paradigm of canonical American fiction to include females in relationships
that were once exclusively male. In *A Prayer for Owen Meany*, for example, Irving pointedly creates a modern Hester to emphasize that the
once ostracized woman is today the vital component in the bond between John Wheelwright and Owen Meany. That Raymond counsels
repudiation of men is a stunning reversal of the current rewriting of
narrative now being practiced by male novelists, a reversal that one
can only describe as ironic in light of the change in male attitudes as
seen in *A Prayer for Owen Meany* and Busch's *Sometimes I Live in the
Country*. Rather than support the redefining, by some contemporary

male novelists, of male bonding to embrace women, Raymond urges the elimination of male bonding altogether: "Gyn/affection, in both its personal and political senses, poses a threat to this oppressive male bonding. It undermines the potential for and the potency of homo-relations" (11). For the sake of female bonding Raymond even goes so far as to call for the banishing of all men, male doctors included, from the delivery room so that the birth of a child may be a "woman-centered event."

The lesser issue here is lesbianism, or what Raymond calls the affinity between Gyn/affection and lesbianism. The greater issue is social strength, for Raymond all but limits female bonding to an urge for political power "to break the stranglehold of hetero-relations" (14). Lisa Alther treats these issues much more sensitively in her novel *Other Women*, but the point remains that in Raymond's account of female bonding sexual preference extends beyond sexual relations to define political status. Yet the affinity described above is far from firm, and thus Raymond distinguishes levels of female bonding between the affirmation of Gyn/affection and the genital experience of lesbianism. In either case her catchphrase is "woman-hating society," a phrase that indirectly suggests her true concern is not only an investigation of bonding among women but also a justification for the denigration of males.

Raymond establishes an opposition between female friendship and hetero-relations, and she insists that the latter is "an overriding theory of oppression" (22). Women bond, she argues, not because of biological needs but because of cultural conditions. The key to women's Otherness is its foundation in women's culture. Biological differences between the sexes are not an issue, and male dominance is not an unredeemable given inherited by humanity since the early moments of the race when the sexual division of labor resulted in the contrast between man-the-hunter and woman-the-gatherer. Culture is a construct. Constructs can be changed. Defining her position with such statements as the "utter brutality of women's oppression," she urges female bonding as the political means of neutralizing the cultural power of hetero-relations (22).[5]

Significant to my concerns is Raymond's criticism of the temptation to use bonding among women as a rationale for repudiating the affairs of the quotidian. Bonding with friends does not mean withdrawing from the world:

Any strong and critical reality of female friendship, any mode of friendship that aims to restore power to the word and reality, cannot be created within a dissociated enclave of women who have little knowledge of or interest in the wider world. Women's friendships cannot be reconstituted in a vacuum of dissociation from the wider world. Any women's community that dissociates itself from a wider world cannot take the place of a wider world. (155)

On the one hand, this opinion may be read as a rejection of utopian schemes that require women first to bond, then to separate from patriarchal hegemony. On the other hand, the statement is an indirect, perhaps even inadvertent, comment on canonical American fiction which details how males bond in the wilderness free of the social contract, which, in the novels, is normally equated with matriarchal authority: the school, the nursery, the kitchen, and the bedroom.

The Last of the Mohicans; Moby-Dick; Huckleberry Finn; The Sun Also Rises; Go Down, Moses; Cannery Row; Henderson the Rain King; and *Deliverance* are celebrated novels of male friendship which assume the sanctity of bonding in a territory dissociated from the society of women. Such dissociation is not lauded in novels of male bonding published in the 1980s, but the fact remains that a male lighting out for the territory—or escaping from the Aunt Sallys of this world—is a staple that unifies traditional American fiction by men. Thus, although Raymond rejects for females—and militantly so—a primary thematic innovation in contemporary narratives of male friendship which shows the questers taking the other gender with them, she accepts a major premise of Richard Russo and Padgett Powell *(Edisto)* that the complexities of society are not to be avoided but met, instead, by those who bond. In recent fiction by men the male companions confront society, even while heading into the territory, when they welcome the female. What is ironic, at least in terms of the long history of American, primarily men's, fiction, is that Raymond and male authors reach at least one similar conclusion but feature different genders. Raymond writes, "Radically chosen dissociation from the world is a temptation as women are constantly confronted with a world that men have fabricated" (155). Males would agree, as the conceit of heading west shows, but with this key difference: the world they escape is shaped by women.

III

Despite Raymond's confidence in her politics, the response to Nancy Chodorow's analysis of bonding extends to areas other than the subtleties of Gyn/affection. Much of the debate about female relationships highlights the definition of woman herself. Femaleness is not always a matter of mothers and daughters. Referring primarily to Chodorow, for example, Elizabeth Abel discusses female friendship as more problematical than the complexities of the mother-daughter affinity might initially suggest.[6] Unlike Nina Auerbach, she is concerned with individual friendships, not with what Auerbach calls female communities.[7] Such friendships are not prominent features in nineteenth-century fiction because the conventions of Jane Austen, Charlotte Brontë, and Kate Chopin tend to dismiss female bonding in favor of society's demands that the natural development of the woman is toward marriage. Bonding diminishes when marriage prevails. Recent fiction by women is a different matter. One of Abel's distinctions, debatable though it may be, is between "complementarity" and "commonality" in contemporary fictional female friendships: "This emphasis on complementarity, however, is a misleading by-product of primarily narrative and thematic considerations. Narrative interest encourages the differentiation of the female protagonists, and concern with the fragmentation implicit in the exclusive quality of women's roles makes dividing the female character into different 'friends' an attractive strategy" (415). Abel argues, on the other hand, that in serious contemporary fiction identification—commonality—is more meaningful than complementarity as the psychological force empowering female bonding.

Male bonding is different. As writers from Cooper to Dickey illustrate, male relationships are generally group oriented. The requirements of the group normally absorb the peculiarities of individual bonds, as Melville shows in *Moby-Dick* (1851) with his celebration of the "joint-stock company," which subsumes the bond between Ishmael and Queequeg. In the novels I consider, however, female bonding is not merged with a group but is, instead, elevated to the status of "we." In other words, when women bond in contemporary fiction they tend to focus on each other rather than on the common goal that often characterizes male bonding. As Abel observes, "friendship becomes a vehicle of self-definition for women, clarifying identity through relation to an other who embodies and reflects an essential aspect of the self" (416). This is a primary reason, I suggest, why, in recent fiction by women, female bonding tends to exclude the male.

Those interested in the intricacies of Abel's argument should also consult Chodorow, for Abel questions the latter's insistence that the mother-daughter affinity is the crucial factor in female bonding. For Chodorow males develop by denying the relation to the mother, and thus they are less than adequately suited to satisfying the relational needs of women, who, says Chodorow, desire both bonding with and separation from the mother. Abel's gloss of Chodorow is crucial to her discussion of female bonding: "Chodorow turns this radical assertion of women's centrality to each other's psychic wholeness into an explanation of the urge to mother: through her intense relation with her child, a mother reexperiences her union with her mother. Chodorow's conclusion is certainly plausible, but her course toward this conclusion leads her to underestimate the role of women's friendships in fulfilling the desire for identification" (418).

The issues are complex, but the difference between Chodorow and Abel is clear: the former stresses mothering as the force of female bonding; the latter emphasizes friendship. Women may indeed have closer ties with one another than men have, or not, but the requirements of friendship are at least as formative as the instinct of mothering in the solidification of female bonding. Men pursue knowledge. Women desire intimacy, which they then define as knowledge. The difference between Irving's *A Prayer for Owen Meany*, a novel of male bonding which includes women, and Chase's *During the Reign of the Queen of Persia*, a novel of female bonding which excludes men, illustrates the distinction. The women in the novels I discuss bond in order to turn friendship into a collaboration to determine meaning within experience. In doing so they simultaneously appropriate the male narrative of the quest and reject the influence of men. As Abel notes, "Identification in friendship becomes a means of mutual recognition instead of an obstacle to objectivity, and interpretation turns into a self-reflexive enterprise as each psyche gains definition through relation to the other" (421). The use of bonding with another as a means of individual wholeness is central to *During the Reign of the Queen of Persia* and *Housekeeping*. The influence of the Other shapes the identity of the self.

Sexual commitment, of course, threatens to turn commonality into complementarity. Abel's observation is similar to that of such feminist anthropologists as Sarah Hrdy, who suggests that female bonding is imperfect in situations of competition. Once the bond takes place males tend to stress the group; females long to privilege the self. This distinction may be due in part to the fact that taking care of others has generally been women's role. Assertion of self is a relatively new phenomenon. Thus, when sex becomes an issue in recent women's fiction the men are either expelled from the wilderness in order to protect the female bond *(Anywhere but Here)* or tamed within it *(During the Reign of the Queen of Persia)*. The issue is not conflict, as it is in traditional novels of male bonding, but commonality. The sisters, for example, in Chase's novel and in Meg Wolitzer's *This Is Your*

Life willingly accept the influence of the Other instead of defending the self against it, and thus they thrive in what Abel calls "relational self-definition" (433). Abel concludes: "This concern with collectivity mediates the desire for originality and places women writers in a different historical as well as psychological situation from their male contemporaries" (434)

Judith Kegan Gardiner applauds the argument but questions the conclusion.[8] Responding to Abel's analysis, Gardiner suggests that the distinctions of commonality and complementarity are not discrete but, rather, "shade into one another" and that the standard female relationship is not necessarily based on one woman's being "older and wiser" than the other (436). Chopin's *Awakening* and Wharton's *House of Mirth* differ from many contemporary novels by women because the female relationship is a narrative device to illustrate alternative role choices. Chopin's Edna, for example, resists bonding with Adele Ratignolle or Mlle Reisz because she sees these friends as personifying contrasting solutions to her dilemma. For Gardiner female bonding is not as stable as Abel intimates. Indeed, Gardiner detects a consistently maintained interplay among women in contemporary fiction so that other characters treat the heroines as the same even while they believe themselves to be different. Thus, commonality and complementarity are not so readily distinguishable. In addition, argues Gardiner, "the narrator finds herself not by merging with another woman but by *writing* about another woman. More generally, I believe this permeability between the author and her text characterizes all these novels and defines a particularly female mode in contemporary fiction" (437).

My point is that in canonical American novels by men male bonding is more or less stable. Such is not always the case in contemporary narratives of female bonding. Mothers and daughters, the bases of Chodorow's analysis, simultaneously acknowledge their bond and shrink from the loss of identity which their fusion entails. *Anywhere but Here* investigates this dilemma and illustrates the woman's fear that marriage to a male annuls identity of the self. Complementarity, not commonality, enhances the normal human need of self-identity.

Significantly, Gardiner writes, relationships in female bonding are not always reciprocal: "One woman in each pair is more of a knower; the other one is to be known" (441). Thus, commonality is not so much the issue as that bonding between women involves both freedom and constraint. One is not surprised, then, to find that in recent novels of female bonding—Joan Didion's *A Book of Common Prayer* comes to mind—the woman who longs to know learns about the friend only after her death. Didion's sense of the bond between Grace and Charlotte is clearly ironic, but knowing and being known are nevertheless bonding issues that she explores. Similarly, Gardiner says, "one's mother can only be understood as a separate person after the childhood mother dies, that is, after the daughter accepts the dissolution of the unregainable mother-infant symbiosis" (441). This is a significant statement—one that I find worked out in *Anywhere but Here* and *This Is Your Life*. Meg Wolitzer illustrates Gardiner's insight that, often in contemporary women's fiction, the heroine both frees herself from loss of identity within the bond and liberates her mother to the status of separate person when she discovers photographs of her mother's girlhood. Wolitzer varies this process when she substitutes televised appearances of the mother for conventional photos, but bonding in this instance is still linked to separation.

Despite their differences, both Gardiner and Abel stress that female identity requires relationship, whereas male identity features individuality and what Gardiner calls "self-containment" (442). This is an important distinction for American literature, one that does not ignore the threat to the sense of self which female bonding can generate because of women's tendencies to encourage commonality in relationships. The danger for the self, writes Gardiner, is "in being obliterated or expropriated by the other" woman (442)—thus, the need for the flexibility of both commonality and complementarity. The traditional notion of female nurturing is always an issue in novels of bonding, for a woman's identity is often best sustained in a "community of women" which supports the individual self and the bonded other. Males need not bother to apply for membership in such a collective.[9]

Gardiner's critique of Abel is not so much a fundamental disagreement as an extension. She elaborates even further in "On Female Identity and Writing by Women" when she distinguishes between male and female responses to texts.[10] Her insight—an insight that may be as radical as it is stimulating—is that many female authors construct their novels in such a way as to stress bonding not only between heroines but also among female author, reader, and character. Gardiner hypothesizes that the female author "is engaged in a process of testing and defining various aspects of identity chosen from many imaginative possibilities. That is, the woman writer uses her text, particularly one centering on a female hero, as part of a continuing process involving her own self-definition and her empathic identification with her character. Thus the text and its female hero begin as narcissistic extensions of the author" (357). If Gardiner is correct—and here one thinks of Diane Johnson's *The Shadow Knows* and Hilma Wolitzer's *Hearts*—then she has identified a primary difference between novels of male bonding, which stress the masculine need to escape social restriction and female inhibition, and novels of female bonding, which stress the feminine need to solidify identity by reaffirming the solidarity of women. The female author uses the text to define the self by creating a female hero with whom she bonds. More important, the bonding process also involves the reader, since the woman reader empathizes with heroines bonded to the female writers who have created them: "'Female identity is a process,' and writing by women engages us in this process as the female self seeks to define itself in the experience of creating art. 'The hero is her author's daughter': bonds between women structure the deepest layers of female personality and establish the patterns to which literary identifications are analogous" (361).

Gardiner's challenging analysis both extends Chodorow's psychoanalytical insights and questions Heilbrun's conclusions about female bonding. Stressing Chodorow's point that the mother-daughter bond shapes female identity, Gardiner believes that a woman's experience varies from "every aspect of identity as men define it" (349). This is why she uses a maternal metaphor of authorship to clarify the special bond—special because men presumably do not have similar affinities—that women writers have for both their characters and their readers. The issue here is that differences between male and female bonding processes are not biological but social. Stability and consistency, for example, have long been held up as desirable goals in male development. In *The Last of the Mohicans* the reciprocal relationship between Natty and Chingachgook is unwavering. But Chodorow and Gardiner argue that, to the contrary, process and fluidity are desirable goals in female development. *During the Reign of the Queen of Persia* develops bonding as a matter of becoming rather than as an assumed fact. It is not that male identity is always static but, rather, that female identity is usually fluid.

These conclusions have far-reaching effects in the continuing effort by feminist literary critics to posit the distinctiveness of women's writing. A primary result is that novels stressing a flexible process of identity and bonding do not conform to the male-oriented canon. Female relationships are not worse than but different from male bonding primarily because women form networks of interrelated bonds rather than principal bonds with one or two other females. Judged by the standards of the paradigm, American novels by women may be formally less unified. The notion of the integrated, solid individual is usually male, and men's writing has determined formal standards in American literature. Contemporary women writers often, but not always, find the self-contained identity to be inappropriate to their experience.

Gardiner disagrees with Heilbrun's contention that women novelists traditionally assume "only a man can stand for the full range of human experience, moving through action and quest to achievement or failure" (*Reinventing Women*, 355). Gardiner objects, suggesting that Heilbrun mistakenly equates the "full range of human experience" with the linear structure of the male quest. Gardiner counters that women authors do not err when they avoid such structures but, rather, they "re-create female experience in different forms" (355). That may be so, but one must respond to her insight with the comment "not always." Many contemporary novels of female bonding do not reject the linear male quest plot; they adapt it. In doing so the female authors send women across the border between society and wilderness to bond in an adventure that often necessitates the repudiation of the male. In other words, the classic paradigm is refined instead of dismissed, and female bonding is thus dissected in ways that call attention to its contrast with canonical American fiction.

The traditional narrative of seduction, love, and marriage (such as James's *The Golden Bowl*, 1904) is not a primary structure in the novels I discuss. Neither is the tendency to exclude women *(Moby-Dick)*. Neither is the literary convention of requiring the female to remain in *(Deliverance)* or return to *(The Scarlet Letter)* the settlement on the safe side of the border. More important, neither is the insistence that aggressive women beyond the border die *(The Last of the Mohicans)*. In contemporary novels of female bonding Cooper's Cora lives.

Notes

1. Nancy Chodorow, *The Reproduction of Mothering: Psychoanalysis and the Sociology of Gender* (1978; Berkeley: University of California Press, 1979).

2. For an account of lesbian analysis of these issues, see Adrienne Rich, *Of Woman Born: Motherhood as Experience and Institution* (New York: W. W. Norton, 1976).

3. Laurie Abraham, Mary Beth Danielson, Nancy Eberle, Laura Green, Janice Rosenberg, and Carroll Stoner, *Reinventing Home: Six Working Women Look at Their Home Lives* (New York: Plume, 1991).

4. Janice G. Raymond, *A Passion for Friends: Toward a Philosophy of Female Affection* (Boston: Beacon Press, 1986), 27.

5. For an account of global—as opposed to American—violence against women, see Lori Heise, "The Global War against Women," *Washington Post*, 9 April 1989, B1.

6. Elizabeth Abel, "(E)Merging Identities: The Dynamics of Female Friendship in Contemporary Fiction by Women," *Signs* 6 (Spring 1981): 413–35.

7. Nina Auerbach, *Communities of Women: An Idea of Fiction* (Cambridge, Mass.: Harvard University Press, 1978).

8. Judith Kegan Gardiner, "The (US)es of (I)dentity: A Response to Abel on '(E)Merging Identities,'" *Signs* 6 (Spring 1981): 436–44.

9. For Abel's reply to Gardiner's critique of Abel's essay, see pp. 442–44 at the conclusion of Gardiner's article.

10. Judith Kegan Gardiner, "On Female Identity and Writing by Women," *Critical Inquiry* 8 (Winter 1981): 348.

Chapter Four

Joan Didion, Diane Johnson, and the Novel of Female Bonding in the 1970s

Carolyn Heilbrun's call for writing women's lives has indirectly resulted in the rewriting of men's texts. Determining moments of cultural change is often speculative, but, if one dates the current feminist movement from the late 1960s, then the novels of the 1970s are among the first to register the social upheaval wrought by the revaluation of gender. Joan Didion's *A Book of Common Prayer* (1977) and Diane Johnson's *The Shadow Knows* (1974) are two such novels, fictions that both adapt the linear plot of the male quest and reject the integrated character as a male-oriented construct inappropriate to the contemporary heroine.[1] (One might also consider Judith Rossner, *Looking for Mr. Goodbar* [1975], Elaine Kraf, *Princess of Seventy-second Street* [1979], and Mary Gordon, *Final Payments* [1978]; all offer variations on the point I suggest.) Neither Didion nor Johnson banishes men from the wilderness, although each documents the eccentricities of masculine prerogatives.

The watershed novel of female bonding, Marilynne Robinson's *Housekeeping*, was not published until 1981, but by the turn of the decade women authors were reducing the presence of men in the text as consistently as canonical male writers had earlier neutralized women. *Housekeeping* signals the change, a significant alteration that prompts a reexamination of the literary paradigm, even while it unexpectedly runs counter to revisions in the narrative uses of gender authored by Robinson's male contemporaries. Discussion of Didion and Johnson highlights the contrast between novels of female bonding in the 1970s, which try to accommodate men, and those in the 1980s, for which *Housekeeping* sets the stage, which undermine men as thoroughly as Cooper undervalues Cora.

I

Midway through Didion's *Book of Common Prayer* Warren Bogart advises his former wife Charlotte to watch her language.[2] In one sense the warning also applies to women in general and to Grace, the narrator, as well, for Grace is involved in writing another woman's life. Although she assumes the precision of scientific objectivity, Grace learns in the course of writing her text that words are inadequate to a narrative of Charlotte's disconnected life and violent death. Worse, Grace realizes that her bond with Charlotte is little more than a linguistic construct and that the failure of her text reflects the flimsiness of their tie.

Didion frames the issues of female bonding in layers of irony. Perhaps the central irony in *A Book of Common Prayer* is that Didion controls her language while she shows Grace's and especially Charlotte's words spinning out of control. Uncertain language weakens women's relationships.[3] Didion traces simultaneously the breakdown of female bonding and Grace's struggle to maintain it. Not emotion, or some mysterious instinct of women's affinity for each other, but words, instead, determine the solidity of the bond. Finally, Didion counters Chodorow's understanding of the mother-daughter relation by illustrating first Charlotte's bafflement by and then separation from her wayward daughter, Marin. Grace, the ostensible novelist, is always involved, because she has to manipulate unreliable flashbacks, secondhand reports, and Charlotte's fictionalizing of her own life to write the variations of her failed bond with Charlotte and of Charlotte's disastrous bond with Marin.

Like female novelists of the 1980s, Didion appropriates the male plot of the quest and sends her bonded females into the wilderness—in this case the Caribbean island of Boca Grande—but, unlike her recent peers, she does not repudiate the male. Grace balances her husband's legacy and her son's politics; Charlotte desires two former husbands whom she alternatively pursues and deserts. Thus, Didion also joins the male novelists of the 1980s in rewriting the paradigmatic American tale to include both genders in the territory beyond conventional restraint. Although surely a celebrator of independent women and female power, she accepts a masculine presence in what might be called the feminist moment.

Language, not gender politics, influences the complexities of

bonding in *A Book of Common Prayer*. Didion speaks indirectly to theoretical concerns that have engaged American and Continental feminist
commentators. Margaret Homans, for example, usefully glosses general differences between literary critics in France and in the United
States.[4] Noting that French theorists posit language and experience as
coextensive, an equation that requires women's silence since language
is a male construct, Homans shows how American critics, in contrast,
assume language to be separable from experience, a distinction that
allows women to speak their own forms of representing the self.
Clearly, the latter theoretical position is more pragmatic. As Homans
observes, "Concerned more with the gender of the text than with the
gender of the writer, the French theorists are not primarily interested
in readings of women authors" (187). One result of this distinction is
that American critics emphasize the need for revising the canon and
rereading misread texts. What all this means to recent women novelists
is that language *is* adequate to the business of communicating the
intricacies of women's experiences. Joan Chase and Mona Simpson,
for instance, recognize that not a new language but a new reading of
the old language is the task before them. Homans argues that "the
advantage of a faith in representation is that even if it offers a delusion,
it is an enabling one. Disbelief in the adequacy of language leads
either to abandoning any attempt to represent women or to settling
for a textual femininity that may bear no relation to actual women"
(190).

Yet—and this is an important demurral—even women authors who
accept the capability of language to represent experience and the self
address, in Homans's words, "women's exclusion from language as
one of their significant themes" (190–91). The result is not only that
French theoretical concerns are relevant to American female writers
but also that American novelists concede, however indirectly, uneasi-
ness about the sufficiency of language, even while they assert its adequacy to communicate their lives as Other.[5] My point is that alternative
modes of expression to male-dominated discourse both facilitate and
threaten the struggle for the female voice in fiction.

Didion's irony is that she asserts the adequacy of language to tell
her tale yet documents Grace's growing disbelief in the accuracy of
linguistic forms. Language may be a male structure, but females can
revise the text. In *A Book of Common Prayer* Didion suggests that the
success or failure of the revision affects the nature of the female bond.
Disillusioned, sixty years old, and committed to science, Grace turns
from anthropology to biochemistry in an effort to rely on facts. The
problem with life and language, she fears, is what she terms "extenuat-

ing circumstances," the undefinable nuances that lie just the other side of the ability of language to communicate the complexities of a life. The external facts of Grace's bond with Charlotte derive from their sojourn in Boca Grande, but the internal uncertainties depend on Grace's ability to shape her text of Charlotte's adventure. Grace abandons anthropology, a discipline that deals in informed speculation, and accepts biochemistry, a discipline that features what she hopes are the hard elements of truth, because she realizes that the realities of her bond with Charlotte are not explained by the notation of biographical facts:

> She made not enough distinctions.
> She dreamed her life.
> She died, hopeful. In summary. So you know the story. Of course the story had extenuating circumstances. . . .
> Give me the molecular structure of the protein which defined Charlotte Douglas.
>
> (3, 5)

These lines from the beginning of the novel illustrate Didion's sense of the tenuousness of both female bonding and the language that would express it.

Charlotte fails with her life, and Grace thinks she fails in relating the extenuating circumstances that determine Charlotte's experience. Didion succeeds, of course, because she understands that her two female characters represent the contemporary woman's opposing responses to language: Charlotte believes that words are a faithful transcription of reality; Grace sees words as endless ambiguities. This is why Charlotte leaves America for the wilderness of Boca Grande. She thinks the literalness of a Third World country will stabilize the flightiness of her life. Grace understands Charlotte's need: "Almost everything in Boca Grande describes itself precisely as it appears, as if any ambiguity in the naming of things might cause the present to sink as tracelessly as the past" (9). Since Grace equates experience with uncertainty, she despairs of ever being what she calls a "witness" to the woman in the bond.

Patriarchal authority, represented by the passport office, limits Charlotte's humanity by defining her with the words *tourist* and *mother,* but Grace senses that a woman's quest is an internal story free of the language that delineates it. The question is how to know the interior of the female experience when all one has to describe it are words. Charlotte has never been at home with language and, thus, is always at sea in her life. She speaks to tourists who are not tourists. She asks for messages that do not come. She writes articles that are not published. She waits for airplanes that do not arrive. She speaks a Spanish that few understand. She reads about subjects that do not interest her. She talks constantly but does not communicate because she uses the clichés of the most "lyrical" day, the most "devoured" meal, the most "hilarious" joke. Lost to a language dominated by men who, in *A Book of Common Prayer*, appear to play at nothing except politics and power, Charlotte reverts to misusing words: "She used words as a seven-year-old might, as if she had heard them and liked their adult sound but had only the haziest idea of their meaning" (29).

One of Didion's many ironies in her narrative of a frustrated female bond is her adaptation of Ernest Hemingway's pared-down language of masculine authority to parody his notions of male power: "Antonio was always handling guns, or smashing plates" (36). The simple grammar of subject-verb-object, made famous by Hemingway, and sardonic sentence fragments illustrate the legacy of the masculine narrative that Charlotte and Grace must cope with and women writers revise if they are to succeed in rewriting the text of American literature. One might even suggest that Didion gives control of the tale to a heroine, then names her Grace in order to reassign Hemingway's famous notion of "grace under pressure" to the other gender.

Didion's larger point is that separation from language means ignorance of history. Charlotte lacks what Grace calls a "specific" history because males have determined it for her. Her first husband, for example, teaches a seminar on *Moby-Dick*, one of the paradigmatic novels of male bonding and masculine heroics, but Charlotte fails her research paper on Melville.[6] When she considers history at all she thinks of male adventure, but she is as isolated from it as she is incapable of using language:

> She understood that something was always going on in the world but believed that it would turn out all right. She believed the world to be peopled with others like herself. She associated the word "revolution" with the Boston Tea Party, one of the few events in the history of the United States prior to the westward expansion to have come to her attention. She also associated it with events in France and Russia that had probably turned out all right, otherwise why had they happened. (57)

Grace's relationship with Charlotte is largely based on the uses of language, except that the former acknowledges a slipperiness that the latter ignores. This is why Charlotte cannot speak of death. Aware that she is dying of cancer, Grace confronts the word *death*, but enunciation of a word does not communicate the circumstances behind it:

It is a little more than a year now since Charlotte Douglas's death
and almost two years since her arrival in Boca Grande.
Charlotte Douglas's death.
Charlotte Douglas's murder.
Neither word works.
Charlotte Douglas's previous engagement.

(52)

Grace and Charlotte meet through language, but only one of them
understands the inadequacy of words.

Grace's effort to write another woman's life revises the canonical
text and renews the bond. Note how she concedes two areas of mutual
concern with Charlotte despite their differences: "On those pages she
had tried only to rid herself of her dreams, and these dreams seemed
to deal only with sexual surrender and infant death, commonplaces of
the female obsessional life. We all have the same dreams" (53). The
"we" includes all women. Aware that, except for twenty years, "Charlotte Douglas's time and place and my time and place were not too
different," Grace realizes that in trying to understand Charlotte she
hopes to write herself before she dies (57).

Her tenuous bond with Charlotte, a relationship that finally
breaks when Grace admits her text has failed to be Charlotte's witness,
is reflected in the dissolution of the mother-daughter bond. Grace
treats her own son with bemused disdain because of his involvement
in the masculine realms of power politics and revolutionary scheming,
but Charlotte's daughter, Marin, is a different matter and more significant to Didion's investigation of language and bonding. Doting on
Marin, holding her hand, Charlotte is baffled by the young woman to
the extent of attempting to rewrite the narrative of their experience
together when the daughter overthrows the mother's values and becomes a political radical (whom Didion models on Patty Hearst). Grace
sees Marin as yet another woman lost to the nuances of language and,
therefore, to the implications of history. Repudiation of the male text
is useless when revision is possible, but neither Charlotte nor Marin
knows realistically how to revise. The mother blithely alters the words
"realistic but optimistic" to "realistic and optimistic" because she prefers the latter. The daughter rejects such alterations but is similarly
divorced from language: "Marin would never bother changing a phrase
to suit herself because she perceived the meanings of words only
dimly, and without interest" (65).

Didion's account of the disintegration of female bonding suggests
that deterioration of the mother-daughter affinity indirectly affects
adult relationships. Mother and daughter in *A Book of Common Prayer*

reflect Nancy Chodorow's psychoanalytic findings about the failure of the one bond that she considers central to female experience. A mother's continuity with her daughter may expand to the extent that connection overwhelms separateness. Chodorow argues that "empathy and primary identification, enabling anticipation of an infant's or child's needs, may become an unconscious labeling of what her child ought to need, or what she thinks it needs. The development of a sense of autonomous self becomes difficult for children and leads to a mother's loss of sense of self as well."[7] In Chodorow's terminology Charlotte fails to reproduce mothering because she defines the mother-child bond according to her own requirements. Aware of the frailty of bonding, Grace advises her readers not to overestimate the possibilities of female relationships. When, for example, Charlotte tells Grace that she and Marin are inseparable, Grace addresses the reader directly: "Accept those as statements of how Charlotte wished it had been" (110). Charlotte's error is that she extends what Chodorow terms "empathy and primary identification" even to conversations with Marin:

> During such periods Charlotte would rehearse cheerful dialogues she might need to have with Marin. For days at a time her answers to Marin's questions would therefore strike the child as weird and unsettling, cheerful but not quite responsive. "Do you think I'll get braces in fourth grade," Marin would ask. "You're going to love fourth grade," Charlotte would answer. (111)

With such a warped notion of bonding the inevitable result is loss of Marin to linguistic triteness and historical ignorance.[8] Charlotte is oblivious to the text. Marin recognizes it because she reads her mother, but when she breaks the female bond she mistakenly tries to repudiate the narrative rather than revise it. She attempts, in other words, to write a totally new text, but, having only old words to use, she can shape nothing but a narrative of cliché:

> "Classic," Marin Bogart said. "Absolutely classic."
> "How exactly is it 'classic.'"
> "Birth control is *the* most flagrant example of how the ruling class practices genocide."
> "Maybe not *the* most flagrant," I said. . . .
> A daughter who never had much use for words but had finally learned to string them together so that they sounded almost like sentences.
> A daughter who chose to believe that her mother had died on the wrong side of a "people's revolution."

(217)

Of all the women in the novel only Grace asserts the futility of separating oneself from responsible narrative, but this is because she is a narrator who recognizes the female need to write women's lives. The inability to manipulate language in a rational way negates one's sense of self. Significantly, Didion does not follow the lead of such militant commentators as Janice Raymond and imply that women are a monolithic force for goodness.

Neither are men, but, unlike some female novelists of the 1980s, Didion does not turn men back from the wilderness. Unlike the heroines of *Housekeeping* and *During the Reign of the Queen of Persia*, Grace and Charlotte expect men in their lives and would like to include them in the bond. Yet the males fail the bonding process as radically as Charlotte and Marin do. Charlotte may live with a husband who cares for her, but he is usually absent, on the phone or on a plane to counsel revolutionaries. A lawyer by profession but a gunrunner by trade, he is Didion's parody of the adventuring male who dispenses law and justice on the quest to power and glory. Yet he brings a framework to Charlotte's life because he is not ignorant of language. Neither is her first husband, who still desires her and whose life revolves around skillful manipulation of repartee. Charlotte leaves both men periodically, but casting off her past leaves her drifting in the present.

For Didion the failure of men to consider women's time as something other than linear destabilizes a woman like Charlotte. Grace remarks, for instance, that, after a meeting with Charlotte's first husband, she "began to see a certain interior logic in her [Charlotte's] inability to remember much about those last months she spent with him" (175). Yet Grace also understands that a female separated from sequential time, even if male defined, is dissociated from life. Note her deadpan account of Charlotte's resistance of the husbands who would shape her life after she journeys to Boca Grande: "She knew what she was going to do. She was not going to do what they wanted her to do. She was not even sure what they wanted her to do but she was not going to do it" (179). Grace, on the other hand, resists the lure of dissociation of the genders. The violent men around her expect women to be intuitive or emotional or nurturing.[9] She rejects the role without rejecting men.

Yet Didion finally argues that neither male nor female models of explaining experience are effective. Late in the novel Grace articulates the affinity between the use of language and the examined life. Commenting on a grammatically scrambled essay that Charlotte has tried to write, she observes, "It occurred to me that I had never before had so graphic an illustration of how the consciousness of the human organism is carried in its grammar" (238). She knows how to make models of life, "DNA, RNA, helices double and single and squared," but when she tries to create the model of Charlotte Douglas that is her text she sees only a shimmer (218). Grace correctly reads the language of an impending coup and leaves Boca Grande to write her tale, but Charlotte disputes the grammar to suit her own needs, remains behind, and dies. At the end of *A Book of Common Prayer* both Grace and Didion are ironic about narrative when they speak to the reader:

> In summary.
> So you know the story.
>
> (279)

But one does not know the story because empirical evidence is always equivocal and language is always ambiguous. One can only read, but never know, the text. In the fiction of Joan Didion the female bond breaks down for similar reasons: self can see but not know Other. It cannot even know self.

II

Diane Johnson agrees. Reviewing *A Book of Common Prayer*, she comments on Didion's negative reaction to the current pressure to write "as a woman":

> To be a woman writing, like a woman directing, is to be expected to have a position toward woman's lot, whether she has one or not, and any book falling from the hand of a woman, however it may have been conceived in purist androgyny (even if that were possible or desirable), will be perceived by reader and critic in the light of the author's womanhood. . . . it is not surprising that Didion has tried to avoid the intensely subjective mode that seems to predominate in recent fiction by women.[10]

In *The Shadow Knows*, Johnson's superb tale of female obsession and shattered bonds, she alludes in the title to the uncertainty of knowing.[11] Those familiar with American popular culture will recognize the reference to the once famous radio program "The Shadow," which echoed weekly the following refrain: "Who knows what evil lurks in the hearts of *men*. The shadow knows" (my emphasis). Johnson's narrator, N., however, goes further than allusions to pop culture, for by the end of the novel N. realizes that evil is a matter not of gender but of humanity.[12] Always unidentified but invariably potent, both men and women terrorize her.

Like Didion, Johnson traces the severing of the female bond, which, for N., occurs when she steps across the border between upper middle-class suburbia and the tangle of a lower-class housing project following a divorce. Both *A Book of Common Prayer* and *The Shadow Knows* illustrate that in the 1970s women's novels of bonding often imagined females embarking on the male quest of adventure but longing to include men in the bond that would sustain them. N. may reject her husband, but, like Charlotte, she nevertheless loves men, who in turn inevitably let her down. So do women. N. learns to her shock that women undermine female relationships—that, as Sarah Hrdy observed during her anthropological research, females react selfishly in an atmosphere of competition.

Significantly, Johnson never names N. except by the initial, which suggests that N. lacks self-definition once she walks into unknown territory. Although Didion's narrator has more assurance than N., the two writers of women's lives resemble each other in their commitment to language. Young, beautiful, and always aware of the effect of her blond hair and large breasts on men, N. is a graduate student of linguistics and, thus, a woman who refuses to abandon the intricacies of language even if they are determined by males: "I sit at my table trying to write the paper. Whether a transformational grammatical solution is applicable to a problem in historical linguistics: the coincidence of Middle English long open 'E' in early Modern English with the reflexes of Middle English long 'A'"(25–26). But N. discovers that such arcane sleuthing in her intellectual life has little to do with the riddles of her daily affairs: someone slashes her tires, telephones her in the middle of the night, ruins her front door, strangles a cat, and beats up her maid. N.'s return to school is seen by her husband as a desertion of domestic duties, which he defines as female, but N. is more concerned with the contrast between the study of language as a scholarly pursuit and the use of language as an indicator of the real: "There seem to be no words to express much of my experience of life, except love and panic" (48).

Her fear is based on the question of whether the mysterious acts of violence are random or related. On the one hand, brutal events are a daily occurrence in housing projects; on the other hand, the terror against her happens too regularly to be accidental. Johnson frames the mystery in a larger question: What happens to a wife and mother when the man who defines her life leaves? Until the divorce N. has refused to acknowledge the shadow, preferring to enclose intelligence, imagination, and emotion in the artificial construct of patriarchal protection, because she has been raised that way. But now the shadow stares her in the face. With the male gone the female is free to write herself. Johnson traces a woman's effort to know her self in the wilderness of unknown vision.

The word *vision* in this context is not too strong. Johnson investigates the obviously flawed, but always persistent, culturally determined dichotomy between the rational male and the intuitive female. N.'s former husband is an attorney (as is her lover), and in *The Shadow Knows* men are represented by lawyers, police inspectors, and judges—in short, by law. Women, on the other hand, are characterized as servants (Ev, Osella), entertainers (Osella), therapy patients (Bess), and divorcées (N.)—as those traditionally in need of law. Cast loose from daily contact with male-determined statutes once she is divorced, N. unexpectedly glimpses "the terror of the real beneath the form" (66). She looks in the mirror and watches the shadow leer back. The formulas of transformational grammar are not going to be much help.

Like her male counterparts in the canon, N. takes a bonded companion with her into the wilderness. Johnson pointedly alludes to the paradigmatic American novel in two ways. First, N., a white woman, bonds with Ev, a black woman and, thus, of a different race, as are Chingachgook, Jim, and Sam Fathers. Second, N. suggests Ev as a female Queequeg because Ev is scarred with razor cuts carved by her lover (24). N. also has ties with Osella, who cares for her children prior to Ev's arrival, and Bess, who serves as her confidante: "We do our best here, Ev and I. We are allies, and love a lot of the same things—men and children and pretty clothes" (14). Males are not excluded from the female quest—no matter that none of the men is the equal of the women. But the bond of mixed gender which retains stability in contemporary fiction by males breaks down in the murky world of *The Shadow Knows.* As N. remarks, "We have to expect reverses sometimes, I guess" (14). They get them. One can hardly overestimate the importance of the following comment when N. explicitly differentiates the inviolability of the male bond from the tenuousness of the female tie: "And then, of course, women will do each other in, I am guilty of that myself; men are loyal to each other and women will do each other in" (116). Johnson shows that males honor the bond, whether in the canonical novel when they keep women out or in contemporary fiction when they include women. Females eventually turn on each other in *The Shadow Knows:* Osella telephones N. late at night with contrasting threats of accusation and silence; Osella severely injures Ev in a surprise attack; Bess slashes N.'s front door and denounces her with hatred.

Or so N. and the reader think. Culpability is never quite clarified because Johnson establishes as a feature of N.'s adventure plot her freedom from definite cause and effect, which is associated with males and from which she is all but separated when her husband divorces her. N. does not judge men as Other, but she understands that males see females as strange. When she speculates that the Famous Inspector will scorn her terror, she explains: "it is not reason which congeals the wellsprings of the Famous Inspector's sympathy, but that he is a man. It is that inchoate masculine fear they all have . . . that she is not him, she is not even like him but is another creature of another race" (39). Yet Johnson knows that this account of male-female difference is conventional. Her irony—one unexpected in a novel of female bonding—is that N. fears women, not men, as alien. In her description of the relationship with Osella she admits dissolving a bond with a woman who is cast out as irrevocably as she: "That was because I didn't understand her at all, or didn't try. She was an alien to me, so dark and fat. . . . It is as if I did not consider her human, this fellow woman" (43). Females are Other to males, Osella is foreign to N., and N. feels distanced from herself.

Thus, her quest is as much to determine identity as to find her way through the shadowed wilderness of the projects. Her narration is an effort to define her own life, and, although she claims that "you never know . . . there's no way of knowing," she nevertheless seizes the opportunity of the quest to pursue what she calls "the shapes of the real beyond the forms," an opportunity denied her when she was married (9, 65). To seek the shapes is to engage the imagination, a power associated with women in *The Shadow Knows*. Johnson suggests that, if men must constrain reality through law, women can create it through vision. Yet visions can spin out of control, endanger the bonded questers, and shock N. and Ev to their knees. Note the repetition of the word *imagine* when N. assumes that her battered front door must be a sign from her potential murderers: "That is an attack you cannot ignore, upon your citadel and upon your imagination. I cannot imagine that we can keep him out next time. It is all too clear to me. I can even imagine a famous police inspector coming along after we're dead to look at our corpses and photograph the blood splashed around" (10). But she does not call the police about the door, and she refuses to change the phone number following the terrifying calls, gestures that hint that N. is a woman who longs to live out her fantasies. She thinks, for example, about "being killed in some intimate personal way," and she visualizes herself as "always walking along the edge of a knife" (19, 16). Fear, N. learns, is exhilarating, as is the proximity of sex and violence, and she has no difficulty timing the

beginning of her visions to the end of her marriage. Guilt both lacer-
ates and soothes: "if someone is trying to kill you, do you maybe
deserve it?" (20).

The answer in *The Shadow Knows* is no. Even Ev suspects that N.
succumbs to fantasy, to the lure of the imagination (female) beyond
the stolidness of the rational (male)—to traps and trials, in other words,
which are unexpected on the quest. Johnson characterizes N. as a
woman who rewrites the male adventure story that Edna Pontellier
refuses to read when she drowns in *The Awakening*, a turn-of-the-cen-
tury novel in which the female bond similarly breaks. In both novels
children are the complicating factor for the female, who would love
men yet challenge male-defined notions of marriage: men on the job,
women in the home. Johnson consciously alludes to the famous moment in *The Awakening* when Edna explains that she would give her
life for her children but that she cannot give herself:

> Mine was the ordinary misery of mothers of small children. At least, I
> think this misery is ordinary. I can try to express the peculiar desperation
> of being the mother of small children but I doubt if I can make it sound
> serious or do anything beyond alienating the Famous Inspector. Men hate
> to hear about this. . . . You love them [children] but you wish they would
> talk about something you are interested in. . . . You are guilty for every-
> thing that happens. You give yourself up. (38–39)

Rejecting the traditional view that wives are supposed to earn their
keep by nurturing the family, Edna and N. resort to the imagination
to fill the void left by their challenges to culturally conditioned notions
of the self, which N. defines ironically as "wifely love and obedience
and motherly concern" (74). Where Edna dreams of escape with Robert Lebrun, N. longs for commitment from her lover. Chopin and
Johnson recast the American paradigm by arguing that the woman is
the willing adventurer while the man clings to the safety of home.
Similarly, both writers criticize the canonical narrative that requires
the woman who disputes the male plot to die (Cora Munro) or be
expelled (Hester Prynne). Note Johnson's irony: "An adulteress in her
blood, by her nature, must seem worse than an adulteress from prin-
ciple or circumstance. A wanton woman is her own murderer, having
first slain womanliness, delicacy, virtue, isn't that so?" (76). Edna
leaves her husband and must drown. N. revises the literary paradigm
and fears she will be murdered.

The point is that, although writing nearly a century apart, Chopin
and Johnson question Nancy Chodorow's thesis about the reproduction
of mothering. The special bond based on preoedipal affinities does

not hold in *The Awakening* and *The Shadow Knows*. Neither Edna nor N. is willing to be what Chopin calls "a mother woman," that is, a woman who approaches life through her children. N.'s confidante, Bess, for instance, cannot understand N.'s insistence that she would hate her children if she had to find a job for their sakes (114). Such an attitude, Bess believes, threatens the bonding of female solidarity, for most women accept their lives as written according to a male narrative. Johnson even goes so far as to recreate Chopin's Adelle Ratignolle, the ultimate mother woman, in the wife of N.'s lover, who always does her duty, who never asks a question, and whose views on mothering are shaped by her husband and parents: "All the pretty houses are full of women like her" (127).

With Chopin, Johnson imagines a woman who becomes trapped in a man's story that, ironically, alienates her from female relationships when she resists the plot. N. writes her own tale and casts herself as both author and heroine. This is why she studies language: "my hand dragging out slow words across a page with no sense that any of them meant anything" (131). The meaning is different because her plot seems strange. In writing *The Shadow Knows* Johnson rewrites *The Awakening* with the significant, shocking variant that, rather than die, N. is "only" raped.

The variation is nevertheless partly ironic because N.'s bonded companion, and thus her other side, dies instead. Although Ev is mistreated by her lover, her death results from an attack likely inflicted by Osella—women violating the bond with women and thereby substantiating N.'s conclusions about male and female difference. Ev's mugging reflects N.'s rape, a violent indicator that their relationship is based on psychological doubling. Establishing their affinity, Johnson alludes not only to Queequeg and Ishmael but also to Friday and Robinson Crusoe: "Ev and I have only been together about ten months but it seems longer, as it would to shipwrecked persons adrift together. . . . We were like two halves of a mirror" (97, 99). Ev's relative silence frames N.'s narrative voice, and both learn from fearful encounters that experience overwhelms one's ability to express it with language. As N. admits late in her effort to revise women's fictions with words, "linguistics is soothing because it has nothing to do with the real world" (205). Ev's unexpected death proves her point. Unlike Ishmael and Queequeg, a male bond that extends beyond the grave when Queequeg's coffin becomes Ishmael's life buoy, Ev's death severs N.'s relationships with women and isolates her to rewrite the American text by herself.

Thus, when the shadow finally strikes, Johnson's macabre irony is that N. accepts the attack as at least not murder. It is as if N. walks around a mysterious bend during her quest and discovers that the feats of strength and skill normally expected of heroes are not as demanding as she had imagined. In her radical revision of the male adventure Johnson undercuts both the canonical paradigm and the reaction to rape: "I was shaking with terror and amazement, and also with a strange elation. . . . I felt happy. . . . There is a badness to things that satisfies your soul" (253). N. means that her imaginative projections have come true, though not according to the story she had envisioned.[13] Still alive to write her own adventure—and, indeed, determined to do so—she concludes merely by vowing to step more carefully when she next gets out of a car in a dark garage.

The Shadow Knows and *A Book of Common Prayer* suggest that one need not repudiate the male when revising the male plot. The complexities of bonding and quest are as much a part of the contemporary women's novel as of the traditional American tale, but Johnson and Didion offer the unexpected feature that the quester retains her interest in men even while the female bond dissolves. A cynic might respond with the cliché that N., Ev, Osella, Bess, Charlotte, and Grace need to have their consciousnesses raised, but awareness of the mutual attraction of the genders seems more to the point. Such is not the case in many novels written by women in the 1980s.

Notes

1. Victor Strandberg is likely correct when he describes *A Book of Common Prayer* as "one of the landmark novels of the decade." See "Passion and Delusion in *A Book of Common Prayer*," in *Joan Didion: Essays and Conversations*, ed. Ellen G. Friedman (Princeton, N.J.: Ontario Review Press, 1984), 162.

2. Joan Didion, *A Book of Common Prayer* (1977; New York: Pocket Books, 1978), 94.

3. For additional commentary on the connection between language and women's relationships, see Russell Davies and John Hollowell. Davies writes, "In *A Book of Common Prayer*, it's as though she saw, in her mind, connections between the confused, revolutionary future and what one might call the rhythmic, natural chaos of womanhood and felt unwilling to spell them out." "On the Verge of Collapse," *Times Literary Supplement* (8 July 1977): 821. Hollowell comments, "Didion's novels, however, are only superficially about the women or about the trouble; on a deeper level, they are about the making of meaning, and the writer's inability or unwillingness to do just that." "Against Interpretation: Narrative Strategy in *A Book of Common Prayer*," in *John Didion: Essays and Conversations*, ed. Ellen G. Friedman (Princeton, N.J.: Ontario Review Press, 1984), 164.

4. Margaret Homans, "'Her Very Own Howl': The Ambiguities of Representation in Recent Women's Fiction," *Signs* 9 (Winter 1983): 186–205.

5. Homans discusses Toni Morrison's *Sula* (1973), Alice Walker's *Meridian* (1976), and Margaret Atwood's *Surfacing* (1972) to illustrate her concerns.

6. Didion also indirectly alludes to *The Great Gatsby*, another canonical text of male bonding. See the essays by Strandberg and Hollowell (cited in nn. 1 and 3).

7. Nancy Chodorow, *The Reproduction of Mothering: Psychoanalysis and the Sociology of Gender* (1978; Berkeley: University of California Press, 1979), 211–12.

8. For an account of mother-child imagery in *A Book of Common Prayer*, see Strandberg's essay (cited in n. 1).

9. Lynne T. Hanley usefully discusses the relationship between *A Book of Common Prayer* and *Salvador*, Didion's account of war in Central America, as a woman author's effort to know the male experience of war. "To El Salvador," *Massachusetts Review* 24 (Spring 1983): 13–29.

10. Diane Johnson, "Hard Hit Women," *New York Review of Books* (28 April 1977): 6.

11. Diane Johnson, *The Shadow Knows* (1974; New York, Vintage, 1982).

12. Muriel Haynes comments on the radical nature of *The Shadow Knows:* "You could say that Diane Johnson is a case of benign neglect. . . . The times should catch up with Diane Johnson now, with the publication of *The Shadow Knows* and the fading of the popular stereotypes about women in general and women writers in particular." "What Evil Lurks . . . ," *Ms.* 3 (November 1974): 37.

13. Inexplicably, there is virtually no scholarship on *The Shadow Knows*, but the rape scene caught the attention of the reviewers. Muriel Haynes writes, "This may very likely be the first novel you read in which rape is cathartic. I warned you, Diane Johnson is the born enemy of received opinion." "What Evil Lurks," 40. Thomas R. Edwards comments, "And it's a sign of the novel's tough independence of outlook that N.'s experience should culminate in an act of casual rape that's treated not as the ultimate affront to her womanhood but as a curious source of relief, showing N. that enmity is real, not imaginary, and also probably impersonal." "Academic Vaudeville," *New York Review of Books* (20 February 1975): 35.

Chapter Five

Revising the Paradigm: Female Bonding and the Transients of *Housekeeping*

The male that Joan Didion and Diane Johnson hope to accommodate in the novel of female bonding is eliminated in the first pages of Marilynne Robinson's *Housekeeping* (1981). When the grandfather's train plunges into the lake to be lost forever in the Freudian waters of femininity, women, in the various guises of mothers and daughters, first try to assimilate the tradition before deciding to rewrite the text. Although *Housekeeping* is Robinson's first novel, its portrayal of female relationships presages a general shift in women's fiction of the 1980s. *Housekeeping* is, in short, a turning point in American literature. Yet to acknowledge Robinson's innovation is not to suggest that she repudiates the male canon. The response by critics is of such variety that a discussion of the highpoints in terms of my own readings of the novel will suggest the complexity of bonding when the canonical text is rewritten.

I

In 1979 Carolyn Heilbrun described the general absence of women's experiences from canonical literature. Observing that the independent male accepts the lure of the quest as the legacy of manhood, she wrote, "Women have avoided adventure, risk and opportunity because they have been taught that suffering, the shaking loose of the comfortable foundations of one's life, must be avoided at all costs.[1] If the female joins Natty Bumppo and declares independence by extricating herself from social restraint, she either suffers with Hester Prynne or dies with Edna Pontellier. Fiction, culture, and gender are inextricably entwined. Heilbrun continued:

All societies, from the earliest and most primitive to today's, have ceremoniously taken the boy from the female domain and urged his identity as

a male, as a responsible unfeminine individual, upon him. The girl undergoes no such ceremony, but she pays for serenity of passage with a lack
of selfhood and of the will to autonomy that only the struggle for identity
can confer. (104)

In other words, the crisis of identity which Huck faces when he decides to "go to hell" or Nick Adams suffers when he refuses to fish
the swamp or Ike McCaslin feels when he finally sees the bear is not
a shock to be avoided but an experience to be embraced. The male
always steps toward knowledge of the self. Such rites of passage inevitably take place away from home and hearth.

To urge the heroine toward the quest is to write her into the
paradigm. Contemporary female authors are changing the canon not
by inventing new forms; rather, they are rewriting old texts. Marilynne
Robinson is very much aware that, in agreeing with Heilbrun's dismissal of the female's "serenity of passage," she also accepts the canonical form of the predominantly male tradition as the foundation
for her ground-breaking novel. Three years after the publication of
Housekeeping Robinson wrote:

> If to admire and to be deeply influenced are more or less the same thing,
> I must be influenced most deeply by the 19th-century Americans—Dick-
> inson, Melville, Thoreau, Whitman, Emerson and Poe. Nothing in litera-
> ture appeals to me more than the rigor with which they fasten on problems
> of language, of consciousness—bending form to their purposes, ran-
> sacking ordinary speech and common experience, rummaging through
> the exotic and recondite . . . always, to borrow a phrase from Wallace
> Stevens, in the act of finding what will suffice.[2]

The word *finding* is significant here, for it suggests the very quest that
the canonical writers used to shape American culture. One year later
Robinson specifically pointed to *Moby-Dick* as a major text of male
bonding and adventure: "I'm a great admirer of nineteenth-century
American fiction and I've been told that *Moby-Dick*, for example, is a
'man's book'—all of which led me to think that if *I* would write a book
with only female characters that men would read, then I could have
Moby-Dick! . . . And, to be honest about it, men have been very nice
about *Housekeeping*. Amazing numbers have read it."[3]

Although a novel of female bonding consciously structured to
appropriate the male text, *Housekeeping* was not reviewed as an indicator of cultural change when it was published. The first reviewers said
little about the growing bond between Ruth and Sylvie or the disinte-
grating tie between Ruth and Lucille in the context of *Moby-Dick* or

similar highpoints of the American tradition. The *Nation*, for example, described *Housekeeping* as "psychological self-mutilation" because Ruth's voice offers no alternative to its "despairing nihilism," and the *Times Literary Supplement* read the novel as an acceptance of transience.[4] Since its first publication, however, *Housekeeping* has been the focus of extraordinarily diverse critical opinion.

Robinson's novel is *the* transition between tales of female bonding in the 1970s as written by Didion and Johnson and those in the 1980s as written by Simpson and Chase. The former illustrate the new women's fiction, fiction that accepts the male adventure plot by rejecting the female's "serenity of passage," that sends bonded women into the wilderness, and that tries to accommodate male presence on the quest. The latter novels generally accept these premises, except for the unexpected rejection of the male even while the female bond is shown to be shaky at best. Still, one does not want to claim too much for *Housekeeping*. In their enthusiasm for the novel some readers tend to regard it as a radical innovation bordering on the unique.

Dana A. Heller is one of the few commentators who locates Robinson's novel in—instead of opposed to—the tradition of the American literary quest.[5] Many discussions of *Housekeeping* questionably place it against what is assumed to be a male notion of the solitary adventure on the far side of the border between society and the unknown. Heller argues that "Ruth and Sylvie's dispossession from the male legacy of isolated heroism enables them to share a destiny of mutual heroic agency and female solidarity. Their commitment to one another both defies the conditions of the male questing pattern and redefines the notion of human agency to include relational capacity" (95). To suggest, however, that the male novelists of the paradigm ignore "relational capacity" is to misread. The heroes of the American text are not solitary but bonded. Indeed, their survival in the territory depends on the solidarity of their relationships. One cannot imagine Natty without Chingachgook, Ishmael without Queequeg, Huck without Jim, Ed Gentry without Lewis Medlock. Their heroism is joined, not isolated. Rather than assert Ruth and Sylvie's "dispossession from the male legacy of isolated heroism," one might better point out that the two women repossess a literary and cultural tradition from which heroines have long been denied. Similarly, Heller writes that "the difference, indeed, is the discovery that a woman's quest—unlike the classic male quest—is not measurable by any resolution reached, grail attained, or dark region overcome" (104). While such a definition may describe the "classic" male adventure, it does not apply to the American tale. A standard feature of American texts of male bonding is lack of closure, failure to find the grail. Natty and Chingachgook do not escape the sound of the axes. Ishmael and Queequeg do not kill the white whale. Huck and Jim do not discover freedom. Sal Paradise and Dean Moriarty do not locate Dean's father. Concluding *Housekeeping* by leaving it open-ended, Robinson does not so much defy the male tradition as rewrite it.

Yet, as Heller observes, the unusual combination of poetic vision and adventuresome quest reflects Robinson's effort to revise the canon without becoming entangled in its forms. Revision of narrative conventions illustrates repudiation of social restoration, just as it does for Melville in *Moby-Dick*. This is why Robinson deliberately writes the first sentence of *Housekeeping* to echo Melville's famous opening line: "My name is Ruth."[6] Death of the mother means loss of conventional history and initiation into what Heller calls "the territory of women's absence" (94). Thus, like Ishmael, Ruth has to assert herself as both namer and explorer of her own experience and, by extension, the experience of other women who dare to cross the border. Entering the wilderness, she finds a new space undefined by propriety and form—by the order of housekeeping. Robinson's revision of the novel of male bonding persuades a readership trained in the American canon that the female quest does not preclude the traditional characteristic of woman's nurturing. Ruth's sister, Lucille, may break the bond by remaining behind with the serenity of passage, but Ruth and Sylvie understand that identity is always being discovered. Learning that history and culture are not monolithic straight lines like her grandfather's train, Ruth eventually associates the fluidity of female experience with the huge lake that frames her adventure through the rugged backcountry of the West.

Heller correctly describes the female quest as "a response to the difficulty of recognizing and coming to terms with difference" (97). Only as Lucille veers toward "serenity" does Ruth accept the journey to find meaning not in the official version of her history as written by the town but, rather, in the fragments of her life as certified by experience. To do so is to understand that the absent may be preserved and rewritten in memory—loss of mother, loss of sister, loss of home. If Sylvie teaches Ruth to be, in the current jargon, "subversive," it is because Sylvie illustrates by her own domestic particulars that commitment to housekeeping is acquiescence to stasis. Women who keep house do not quest. To enter the wilderness is to be flexible about boundaries—Huck's river, Ishmael's ocean, Ike McCaslin's big woods—as Sylvie corroborates when she allows the outdoors, in the guise of darkness and leaves, to invade the indoors of her house, much to the shock, of course, of Lucille and the male officials of law, school, and custom. In this way Sylvie leads Ruth to reject the binary oppositions of indoor-outdoor, light-dark, society-nature, and to embrace, instead, a unity based on female notions of fluidity.

Describing Ruth's trip on the lake with Sylvie, Robinson simultaneously recalls and recasts Ishmael's journey with Queequeg on the ocean and Huck's passage with Jim down the river. When the two women stop at an abandoned cabin and Sylvie leaves Ruth alone to pull down the planks of a house, one understands Ruth's repudiation of the long-accepted male equation of the female and the parlor. Huck can't stand "sivilization," which he equates with female propriety. Ruth can't either, except she interprets it as the male text. Burning magazines and books—one of which is *Not as a Stranger*, a tale of a man's betrayal of a woman's sacrifice—Sylvie enables Ruth to rewrite the text, usually male, which traditionally defines culture. This is why Ruth is metaphorically reborn during the journey back across the lake as she sits between Sylvie's legs like a seed, surrounded by water, ready for a new mother, a new self, a new understanding of female power. As Heller shows, the fluidity of femininity guarantees a life of ever-recurring rebirths, a celebration of transience rather than an acknowledgment of stability.

To make these points in summary fashion, however, is not to agree that Robinson's account of female bonding in *Housekeeping* offers what Heller calls "a feminist alternative to the Huck Finns and Sal Paradises of American fiction" (104), as if the text as written by women were in opposition to the text as understood by men. *Housekeeping* rewrites but does not repudiate the paradigm. Robinson is on record as celebrating the great shapers—primarily male—of the American canon, and Joan Kirkby and Maureen Ryan discuss *Housekeeping* within the context of the tradition.[7] They observe, for example, that Robinson alludes to Melville, Dickinson, Thoreau, Emerson, Hawthorne, Poe, Fitzgerald, Franklin, Alcott, Frost, Faulkner, and Jewett. On the one hand, Robinson acknowledges the standard writers of the male quest, for, like them, she excludes the other gender from the bond. One of her ironies is that the shaky relationship in *Housekeeping* is shored up by a woman who, from a traditional point of view, personifies shakiness. On the other hand, she revises the standard male novel, which normally *begins* with the plunge into the wilderness. She rewrites so that the threat to the bond between Ruth and Sylvie precipitates a quest, which *ends* the novel. Reshaping the canonical text, she shows that the heroine is not, as R. W. B. Lewis would say of the hero, "unencumbered."

Strict feminists would speak here of Robinson's subversion; I merely note a recasting of the tradition that white male novelists of the 1980s also stress. One understands that, as concepts of the heroine change, so applications of the paradigm alter. As Ryan observes, "The woman writer who envisions more for her female hero must struggle to transcend readers' expectations about feminine literary behavior" (82). *Housekeeping* provides the means of transcendence for the contemporary novel of female bonding. Ryan points out that Ruth is liberated into family, not from it, as, say, Huck is, although one might also stress that Ruth's family bond is as unconventional as Robinson's revision is unexpected. By concluding with the beginning of the quest as the family of new mother and daughter walks away from civilization, Robinson alters two established, not to say revered, canonical traits: the male expectation that the hero leaves the woman at home and the female expectation that the heroine closes with marriage or death. Like Leatherstocking or Huck or Ike, Ruth learns that to know the self is to reject community.

The conventional family relationship in *Housekeeping*, the one that Cooper, for example, insists on in *The Last of the Mohicans,* is between the sisters Ruth and Lucille. Yet, when Lucille reads the text in the traditional female manner and chooses to break the bond by living with her home economics teacher, Robinson establishes the irony that the female Lucille becomes Other to the new heroine Ruth. Ryan suggests that, in selecting Sylvie rather than Lucille for the bond, Ruth allows Sylvie to offer her "different ways of being female" (84), but one wonders whether femaleness is finally the issue. With Sylvie's help Ruth appropriates the male plot and, thus, revises the paradigm to write a new way of being human, a kind of androgyny which illustrates the rethinking of gender gaps one notes in recent fiction by both men and women. Robinson's freeing of Ruth into family is, in my opinon, not as radical as first appears. Traditional American fiction may show the hero escaping immediate kin, but the hero does not walk the long trail alone. Just as Ruth loses mother and sister but finds a new mother in Sylvie, so Uncas is Natty's son, Jim is Huck's father, Queequeg is Ishmael's brother, and so on through the canon. Robinson deliberately recalls the tradition to write a change within it.

Her decision to allow Ruth to select a mother rather than merely accept the one she is born to challenges long-held notions of the mother-daughter bond. Martha Ravits draws on Chodorow's conclusions and succinctly states the issue:[8]

> Ruth as bereaved quester asserts the primacy of the relation to the mother
> as none of the male orphans so prevalent in American literary history
> before her have done. Ishmael, Huck Finn, Isaac McCaslin undertook
> the struggle for maturity by choosing surrogate fathers. Ruth's quest fo-
> cuses long overdue attention on the individual's resolution of feelings
> about the bond to the mother as the primary, requisite step in the ascen-
> sion to selfhood. For the maturing female hero, it is the mother—missing,
> absent, but always present to the child's imagination—who is the key to
> reality. (648–49)

The scene at the ruined house in the woods when Ruth pulls off the
clapboards is Sylvie's test of Ruth's willingness to look forward instead
of back by defining a new understanding of bonding which precludes
the return of both fathers and mothers. Rather than the male initiation
that requires trial by strength and competition, Ruth undergoes a specifically female rite of passage, which Ravits describes as "a ritual of
rebirth and connection": "The female hero's courage consists not of
physical fortitude tested against external dangers but of courageous
subjectivity in the face of isolation and neglect, inner assaults to selfhood sustained over time" (661, 659). Yet, although Ruth and Sylvie
create a daughter-mother bond before finally crossing the lake to the
wilderness, Robinson rejects the current tendency to idealize female
communion and celebrates, instead, the power of self. Ruth selects a
mother as Huck affirms a father, but heroines and heroes in American
fiction usually learn that the sad cost of selfhood is confrontation with
the unknown.

A question that engages readers of *Housekeeping* is whether Robinson reaffirms Chodorow or redefines the mother-daughter relationship. Marcia Aldrich, for example, refers to Chodorow's findings to
discuss Ruth's bond as a "long continuation of her pre-oedipal attachment to her mother,"[9] but Elizabeth Meese stresses Robinson's distinction between mother and mothering:[10] "Without men and without
mothers, the definitional status of women and family life changes radically" (59). Rewriting Huck's bond with Jim or Ike's with Sam Fathers,
Robinson shows mothering to be more important than mothers. Once
parents are eliminated women define themselves differently, not, as
culture traditionally requires, as merely separate from men, but, instead, on their own terms, free of restrictive conventions that read
women and housekeeping as a metaphor of order in disordered nature.

Like Huck, Sylvie and Ruth understand the expectations of those
who determine social forms, but they consciously undermine the conventions of parenting and housekeeping. Cast free of the biological
mother, Ruth uses Sylvie to create herself out of fear of an anonymity

caused by her being abandoned by the surrogate mothers who should have helped her shape a sense of self. Thus, Ruth recaptures lost notions of mothering by inventing them in her text, by writing, as it were, Sylvie as the missing mother. As Meese observes, "The author shows us what it means for the text to inscribe itself within its readers" (67). By the end of the novel, at the beginning of the quest, Ruth senses that in telling her tale she has written herself: "It had never occurred to me that words, too, must be salvaged, though when I thought about it, it seemed obvious. It was absurd to think that things were held in place, are held in place, by a web of words" (*Housekeeping*, 200). She constructs her story and the bond that sustains it by deconstructing culturally accepted definitions of mothers and heroines. This is why *Housekeeping* ends with Ruth's multiple interpretations of her adventure. Male belief in facts and the stability that shapes them is finally sterile.[11]

Housekeeping suggests that traditional theories of mothering entrap both mothers and daughters. The death of Ruth's grandfather and the subsequent disappearance of males and various mother figures necessitate a new narrative to tell the tale of the tribe, which Ruth begins writing with the very first word of her text: *my*. The search for the father is a continuing plot in canonical American fiction, as illustrated by Jack Kerouac's *On the Road* (1957), which concludes with Sal Paradise remembering "the father we never found."[12] Ruth, however, breaks free of the myth of masculine heroics by beginning with the lost father. Revising the paradigm, she rereads the past to feature the voice of a daughter in search of mothering.

In perhaps the most thoughtful discussion of the complexities of the mother-daughter relationship in *Housekeeping* Phyllis Lassner argues that Ruth and Sylvie form a new bond of femininity which banishes *both* fathers and mothers.[13] Pointing out that *Housekeeping* is a tale not of continuity among women but, rather, of self, Lassner speaks of Ruth and Sylvie escaping the "unfathomable depths of the father's story" and "the pressure of their mothers' examples" (52). To accept Lassner's conclusion, at least for the purposes of discussion, is to read *Housekeeping* as Robinson's indirect challenge of Chodorow's notion of the reproduction of mothering. Robinson's innovation is to show that the mother-daughter bond, as traditionally understood, hinders self because it facilitates mutual absorption to the detriment of the individuals involved. Commenting on Ruth's grandmother aging into an image of mother Eve, Lassner writes, "It is as if motherhood practiced at its most intense level of selflessness pushes women into a retrograde primitive state" (53). Robinson rejects the regression. *Housekeeping* is a watershed in the contemporary novel of female bonding because it defines the standard mother-daughter relationship as restrictive rather than nurturing.

Chodorow argues the need of daughters to reproduce mothering, but Robinson shows Ruth suffering ties to several different kinds of mothers before reading Sylvie as a new definition of the bond based on reciprocity instead of absorption. An enduring bond rejects identification to nurture difference.[14] Fusion with Eve annihilates self. Thus, on the way back across the lake Ruth is reborn between Sylvie's legs to a different sense of being a daughter, a difference that does not negate relationship and yet privileges self. Lassner observes that the only way for Ruth to achieve difference—and to nurture it in Sylvie—is to realize that, contrary to Ruth's initial desire, Sylvie does not reproduce the lost biological mother. The price, of course, is the soul-consuming threat of loneliness—as Leatherstocking, Ishmael, Huck, and Ike McCaslin know. Ruth admits early in the novel that "such a separation . . . could indeed lead to loneliness intense enough to make one conspicuous in bus stations" (*Housekeeping*, 68). The end of *Housekeeping*, like the conclusions of *The Prairie*, *Moby-Dick*, *Huckleberry Finn*, and *Go Down, Moses*, is sad: there is no final garden where the American quester can expect protection in the nurturing bosom of Adam or Eve.

II

The first sentence of *Housekeeping*—"My name is Ruth"—illustrates the enormous difference between novels of female bonding in the 1970s and those that follow *Housekeeping* in the 1980s. Joan Didion, for example, gives her female narrator a first-person voice in *A Book of Common Prayer*, but Grace promptly dismisses the importance of her voice to the tale: "I tell you these things about myself only to legitimize my voice. We are uneasy about a story until we know who is telling it. In no other sense does it matter who 'I' am: 'the narrator' plays no motive role in this narrative, nor would I want to."[15] All but silencing the "I" in the voice, Didion's narrator remains in the wilderness of Boca Grande to reveal more about her bonded companion than about herself.

Such is not the case in *Housekeeping*. Robinson's narrator begins her first sentence with "My" and her second sentence with "I," and one knows from the outset that Ruth claims the right to name herself and to tell her tale. Robinson understands that such prerogatives are traditionally left to the male adventurer. Not Eve but Adam, after all, is the mythical namer in human history. But Ruth usurps the task and, thus, the power to write the story before it gets started without her. Not to do so would be to relegate her voice to the standard narrative of male bonding in the wilderness, for Ruth is raised by women in a house built by a now dead grandfather who believed in the priority of the masculine adventure to the far reaches of the West: "my grandfather began to read what he could find of travel literature, journals of expeditions to the mountains of Africa, to the Alps, the Andes, the Himalayas, the Rockies. . . . One spring my grandfather quit his subterraneous house, walked to the railroad, and took a train west" (3–4). When, years later, the train hurtles from the intimidating bridge across the lake and takes Ruth's grandfather with it, the patriarch is simultaneously eliminated from the territory and established in death as an ironic contrast to Ruth and Sylvie, who will eventually cross the bridge on foot at the end of the novel to begin their quest toward life.

Unlike Richard Russo, Frederick Busch, Larry Woiwode, and other male writers of the 1980s who refuse to banish women from the wilderness and who thereby close the gender gap that has long defined the American canon, Robinson excludes the man as forcefully as Cooper and Melville turn back the woman. Her reopening the gap from the other side, as it were, signals an emphasis on exclusionary female power that other women writers later in the decade of the 1980s exploit in various ways. Eradication of the male affirms the female. Robinson creates an unstable community of women in the Idaho mountains who now look to the surviving grandmother as a matriarch "just returned after an absence" (12). Ruth's voice solidifies female presence. Relieved by the patriarch's death of the need to succeed in the conventional sense, which Robinson defines as male, the women learn that male and female time are not the same: "With him gone they were cut free from the troublesome possibility of success, recognition, advancement. They had no reason to look forward, nothing to regret. Their lives spun off the tilting world like thread off a spindle, breakfast time, suppertime, lilac time, apple time" (13).

Robinson, however, offers nothing so simple-minded as "erase the man to save the woman." Aware of the complexities of bonding and the vagaries of the quest, she suggests at least in the case of Ruth and Lucille that the female bond is often tenuous because women look out for themselves in moments of competition. The matriarch's presence following the patriarch's absence does not automatically affirm Ruth's need to write her own life. Indeed, the grandmother lives the role of the conventional nurturing female, the woman who turns to housekeeping to beat back the night. Her commitment to domesticity encloses the female rather than frees her: "She had always known a thousand ways to circle them all around with what must have seemed like grace" (11). To claim the right to tell her tale—to write, in other words, the word *my*—Ruth must rewrite the nurturing of the grandmother, the memory of the mother, and the bond with the sister. She must not, in short, reproduce mothering. She has a hard time doing so.

Robinson suggests that the mother-daughter bond should be not reproduced but redefined. When Ruth's mother Helen commits suicide in the very lake that holds the grandfather she inadvertently places her daughter in the dilemma of recreating a mother who is forever absent. To look to the grandmother is to acknowledge housekeeping, which, in Robinson's novel, is equated with artificial order and static life. Those who keep house do not write their own lives. The grandmother's response to Helen's death is Ruth's model until Sylvie opens the doors to the leaves and the dark: "she [the grandmother] whited shoes and braided hair and turned back bedclothes as if re-enacting the commonplace would make it merely commonplace again, or as if she could find the chink, the flaw, in her serenely orderly and ordinary life" (25).

Robinson's irony is that Sylvie will personify the chinks and flaws in the traditional cycle of domesticity when she arrives to care for Ruth and Lucille. The sisters expect a reproduction of their mother. What they get is a character of unexpected importance to American literature. Sylvie revises the male role of the wanderer and becomes the Natty Bumppo of contemporary novels by women. Conventional women who fail at mothering because they prefer stiff linens and polished silver to bonding with Ruth describe Sylvie in terms that recall the names of the canonical American literary hero: "'An itinerant.' 'A migrant worker.' 'A drifter'" (31). Ruth and Lucille would be Huck Finn and Tom Sawyer; their great aunts would have them be Becky Thatcher. To acquiesce, however, means that Ruth will write her grandmother's life instead of her own. With comic bluntness Robinson suggests that in the American canon women do not rate even the words of an obituary. When the grandmother dies the local newspaper omits her photograph, neglects to mention the time of the funeral, and features instead the stale story of the grandfather's spectacular death. Sylvie shows Ruth how to rewrite the tale.

Although admitting to a marriage of "sufficient legal standing to have changed her name," Sylvie prefers solitude and transience to husband and housekeeping (43). Her green dress foreshadows the life and leaves she will let into the house, and her penchant for traveling by train to "wherever" signals her appropriation of male wandering previously thought to be the privilege of grandfathers and patriarchs. Robinson dramatizes the complexities of female bonding, however, by refusing to sentimentalize Sylvie as a comic book heroine rushing to the rescue of the all but orphaned sisters. Not Robinson but Ruth idealizes the questing woman as her drowned mother reborn. Raised by a grandmother and two great aunts who honor traditional concepts of mothering and housekeeping, Ruth expects Sylvie to step into the role: "she reminded me of my mother more and more" (53). The resemblance, of course, is inaccurate, more an indication of Ruth's longing than of Sylvie's status. Preoedipal bonds may indeed be as significant as Chodorow argues, but Robinson shows that women are not born but trained to search for reproductions of their mothers. Restrictive rather than liberating, standard mother-daughter relationships keep women perpetually at home. For Ruth to locate a replication of her mother would be to turn her into Lucille.

In Robinson's understanding of women in the wilderness definitions of female bonding must be revised. Living with Sylvie means camping among the leaves with Huck rather than acknowledging Hester Prynne's sewing. The flooding of the town offers Ruth and Lucille an invitation to the quest, a way of rewriting the texts of their mothers. The library is flooded; the needlepoint footstools and braided rugs are ruined; the wedding dresses and photograph albums become moldy. In place of the canonical texts in the ruined library Sylvie tells stories whose unifying detail is a train or bus station. Robinson never hints that boarding the train is easy for the woman who would find a new bond in the territory. The price of leaving home is the threat of loneliness, as when Ruth concedes, following the flood, that "the restoration of the town was an exemplary community effort in which we had no part" (74). More important, Lucille's complaint about tiring of camping in the flooded house is Ruth's first panged awareness that her bond with the sister will not hold.

Celebrating Ruth's redefinition of the mother-daughter bond with Sylvie at the end of the novel, one should recall that Ruth initially honors her allegiance to Lucille when their relationship begins to waver. Rereading is always safer than rewriting. "Reinventing womanhood" means breaking ties with sisters.[16] Robinson rejects such politicized fantasies as female solidarity and illustrates, instead, that Heilbrun's serenity of passage promises security. Most men are not Huck Finn or Ishmael, just as most women are not Sylvie. When, for instance, Lucille takes her first steps toward accepting culture's definition of propriety, Ruth conforms her attitude to her sister's. Lucille is what Ruth calls "of the common persuasion"—that is, a replica of the vast majority of women. Fixing her hair, arranging her room, and fearing the changes of the future, Lucille adopts her mother's sense of housekeeping as the creation of order. To reproduce mothering is, for Lucille, to repress self.

Sylvie, on the other hand, lives in "a millennial present" (94), and through her Robinson shows that the choice for Ruth and all women is between the safety of home, with its fear of the future, and the life of the quester, with its acceptance of now. One might argue that the tie between Ruth and Lucille is tighter than I have suggested because the latter cuts school as often as the former in order to walk the countryside, but Ruth understands that "Lucille went to the woods with me to escape observation. . . . But I went to the woods for the woods' own sake" (99). Only Lucille queries Sylvie about her absent husband—who is a soldier, the epitome of the generic man-the-hunter. Only Lucille begins requesting regular meals, stylish attire, and the elimination of transience—in short, housekeeping. Ruth's fear of becoming like Sylvie is Robinson's sign that severing the tie with the sister—and, thus, breaking the bond with the mother—requires a radical recasting of self.

Robinson indicates that the primary stumbling block to rewriting bonding is the attempt to reprise rather than redefine the mother. To wait, as Ruth does, for Sylvie to "claim" her is to negate the power of self. Such passivity undermines the female's effort to revise the male text. Thus, in a memorable passage Robinson glosses the breaking of the sisterly bond by describing opposing reinventions of the mother's role: "Lucille's mother was orderly, vigorous, and sensible, a widow (more than I ever knew or could prove) who was killed in an accident. My mother presided over a life so strictly simple and circumscribed that it could not have made any significant demands on her attention. She tended us with a gentle indifference" (109). Robinson solidifies these imaginary accounts of mothering when she differentiates between Ruth's and Lucille's responses to the ramshackle shelter they build by the lake. The structure is "random and accidental," periodically collapsing, clearly an affirmation of Sylvie's haphazard housekeeping (114). Lucille sits beside Ruth "in our ruined stronghold, never still, never accepting that all our human boundaries were overrun," but Ruth lets "the darkness in the sky become coextensive with the darkness in [her] skull and bowels and bones" (115, 116). Baptized when she falls in the lake, Ruth joins Sylvie and embraces the Otherness of nature. Lucille tries to sweep it out with a broom.

In Robinson's rethinking of the canon Lucille becomes Tom Sawyer, the upholder of social form, to Ruth's Huck Finn, the defier of established convention. Their bond breaks when Lucille frequents the drugstore with the in crowd while Ruth wanders the woods alone. Yet Robinson argues that such radical separation and loneliness have compensation in the recurring cycles of life if only Ruth will abandon her desire to remake Sylvie in the image of her mother: "It seemed to me that what perished need not also be lost" (124). Ruth may tell her tale and thus hold onto her mother in memory, but Robinson defines the new bond with Sylvie as a means not of reproducing mothering but of releasing self. Lucille searches for the lost mother in the guise of the home ec teacher who codifies housekeeping; Ruth bonds with Sylvie and realizes that, "if I could see my mother, it would not have to be her eyes, her hair. I would not need to touch her sleeve. . . . The lake had taken that, I knew" (159).

The key to Ruth's knowledge and to Robinson's rewriting of women's lives is recognizing loneliness as a means of discovery. Robinson's paradox is that bonding liberates self: "Because, once alone, it is impossible to believe that one could ever have been otherwise. Loneliness is an absolute discovery" (157). What Ruth discovers is that Sylvie can forget Ruth is at her side, can speak to others as if Ruth were not there, can maintain their bond in spite of giving Ruth almost no thought at all. Sylvie is Ruth's new mother but not at the cost of absorbing her into some prescribed whole. Affirming this newly defined relationship means understanding that possession is useless, that nature always overwhelms houses, that "it is better to have nothing" (159).

Their boat trip across the lake initiates their quest beyond the border. Offering Ruth a trial by wilderness, Sylvie tests her awareness of loneliness. Ruth begins the journey by sitting in the boat like "a seed in a husk" (162), but she concludes it by being born to the adventure that traditionally only males have risked in paradigmatic American fiction. Women have always meant time and, thus, the threat of mortality to the canonical hero, a personification of diminishment to be escaped by heading west. In Robinson's revision, however, the heroine is the woman who ignores time. The sheriff and school principal, not Sylvie, watch the clock and worry about Ruth's absences from school. Always assuming the role of namer and law giver, men have erased women from the tale, much as Ruth's grandmother is absent from her own obituary. But Robinson turns a historical absence into a mythical presence when she equates Sylvie with Noah's unnamed wife and sends her across the water: Noah's wife "was a nameless woman, and so at home among all those who were never found and never missed, who were uncommemorated, whose deaths were not remarked, nor their begettings." Men tell what Robinson dismisses as "the tedious tale of generations" (172). Women in the 1980s revise the text.

Ruth's narrative, then, commemorates all the women left behind. By claiming the right to call her own name, by insisting on the word *my*, she alludes to the biblical heroine Ruth and tells the story of those who have had no teller. Robinson celebrates a new understanding of family when she takes Ruth and Sylvie across the bridge to the long adventure that awaits them on the far side of home. No Leatherstocking will be their guide, but women will sing their song: "For families will not be broken. Curse and expel them, send their children wandering, drown them in floods and fires, and old women will make songs out of all these sorrows and sit in the porches and sing them on mild evenings" (194).

As Ruth and Sylvie move toward the bridge to rewrite the canonical American tale of male bonding, Robinson defines *drifting* as "not the worst thing" (210). They join Huck and Tom, for the townspeople think they have drowned, but, unlike Twain's heroes, Robinson's heroines keep drifting west, never reappearing in the houses of their mothers. Ruth remarks that they were "never found, never found," and of course they aren't in the official version of the tale (213). But Ruth's voice revises the fates of her grandmother and Noah's wife. In her revision—a novel called *Housekeeping*—the lost women are always found, free of what she terms "these ceremonies of sustenance, of nurturing," to write women's lives in the strangeness of the wilderness (214). The "perimeters" of their wandering are nowhere, and thus Robinson liberates her bonded females to stride through the canon, reshaping the text as they go (219). In so doing she formalizes the new standard of gender exclusivity which is the hallmark of American women's writing in the 1980s: males are rejected from the bond.

Notes

1. Carolyn G. Heilbrun, *Reinventing Womanhood* (New York: W. W. Norton, 1979) 68.

2. Marilynne Robinson, "So Where Does a Writer's Influence Come From?" *Ms.* (August 1984): 112.

3. "Marilynne Robinson," *Conversations with Contemporary American Writers*, ed. Sanford Pinsker, New Series 50 (Amsterdam: Costerus, 1985), 122.

4. Brina Caplan, "It Is Better to Have Nothing," *Nation* 232 (7 February 1981): 154; Julie Kavanagh, "Escaping into Flux," *Times Literary Supplement* (3 April 1981): 371.

5. Dana A. Heller, *The Feminization of Quest-Romance: Radical Departures* (Austin: University of Texas Press, 1990), 93–104.

6. Marilynne Robinson, *Housekeeping* (1981; New York: Bantam, 1984), 3.

7. Joan Kirkby, "Is There Life after Art? The Metaphysics of Marilynne Rob-

inson's *Housekeeping,*" *Tulsa Studies in Women's Literature* 5 (Spring 1986): 91–109. Maureen Ryan, "Marilynne Robinson's *Housekeeping:* The Subversive Narrative and the New American Eve," *South Atlantic Review* 56 (January 1991): 79–86.

8. Martha Ravits, "Extending the American Range: Marilynne Robinson's *Housekeeping,*" *American Literature* 61 (December 1989): 644–66.

9. Marcia Aldrich, "The Poetics of Transience: Marilynne Robinson's *Housekeeping,*" *Essays in Literature* 16 (Spring 1989): 133.

10. Elizabeth A. Meese, *Crossing the Double-Cross: The Practice of Feminist Criticism* (Chapel Hill: University of North Carolina Press, 1986), 55–68.

11. For a sophisticated reading of *Housekeeping* in terms of Julia Kristeva's theory of "women's time," see Thomas Foster, "History, Critical Theory, and Women's Social Practices: 'Women's Time' and *Housekeeping,*" *Signs* 14 (Autumn 1988): 73–99.

12. Jack Kerouac, *On the Road* (1957; New York: Viking Compass, 1962), 310.

13. Phyllis Lassner, "Escaping the Mirror of Sameness: Marilynne Robinson's *Housekeeping,*" in *Mother Puzzles: Daughters and Mothers in Contemporary American Literature,* ed. Mickey Pearlman (Westport, Conn: Greenwood, 1989): 51.

14. Lassner quotes Mary Jacobus, *Reading Women* (New York: Columbia University Press, 1986), 280. "Without difference there is nothing but freezing identity." See Lassner, "Escaping the Mirror," 54.

15. Joan Didion, *A Book of Common Prayer* (1977; New York: Pocket Books, 1978), 14.

16. The phrase "reinventing womanhood" is Carolyn Heilbrun's.

Chapter Six

Women without Men

Mona Simpson: *Anywhere but Here*

When Marilynne Robinson published *Housekeeping* in 1981, use of first-person voice for an adolescent female narrator in a serious American novel written by a woman was generally considered an innovation because girls were thought to be defined by male structures. Not anymore. In Mona Simpson's *Anywhere but Here* (1986) Ann writes her own life by telling her mother's tale.[1] Simpson has remarked that, contrary to the expectation of some feminists, she deliberately set out to write a quest novel not as a woman's story only but also as a narrative of America:

> With this book, I actually began with an image of a woman on a clean highway, putting her kid outside by the road, driving off and then coming back, the kid standing in the ditch, waiting. . . . The book is about the people who stayed in their hometowns and put down their roots and the people who went west and tried to get more from life, because that seems to me the story of life in America. . . . Adele is unstable, but troubled by American troubles: by the striving for gentility, the striving for a higher station. I wanted her dreams to be what got her into trouble.[2]

Unlike the canonical American narrative, which is often about fathers and sons, *Anywhere but Here* features mothers (Adele) and daughters (Ann) with the significant twist that the mother is far from an exemplary parent. Simpson concedes that she disliked Adele when she first created her. Readers are likely to agree: Adele is no Sylvie *(Housekeeping)*. One might even read *Anywhere but Here* as an account of what happens to bonded women after they cross Robinson's bridge. Detailing Ann's adventure with Adele from childhood to college, Simpson uses the tensions of the mother-daughter relationship to explore the darker side of the American need to head west in order to convert dreams into life. Surviving in the territory beyond home is just as problematical in contemporary fiction as it was in the day of Leatherstocking and Chingachgook.

As Ann describes the bond, she shows it to be a compilation of love, hate, and canonical fiction. *Anywhere but Here* is a road novel as *Housekeeping* is not, and one recalls *On the Road* when Adele drives Ann toward California in a stolen, white Lincoln Continental. In flight from other mothers, distant homes, Simpson's questers accept the pattern for the novel of female bonding established by Robinson and immediately banish men from the journey. Adele and Ann welcome men sexually as Ruth and Sylvie do not, and Adele dreams of catching the perfect husband created in her fantasy of what a husband ought to be, but no man measures up to the strictures of their bond. The lack of males is, of course, deliberate on Simpson's part, as if writing women's lives means erasing men's presence. Of the reviews I examined only Le Anne Schreiber remarks on the impact of this absence: "There is an evasion, an absence, at the heart of this novel. What's missing—from Ann's life, from the recollection of Adele's girlhood, from the women's reckoning of their relations to one another—is fathers. Fathers are mentioned, yearned for, their now distant deaths and departures mourned, but mostly they are a silence, a secret the women keep from one another."[3]

At issue is not the male-male bond, as in the paradigmatic American novel, or the male-female relationship, as in the traditional novel of marriage and home, but the affinity between mothers and daughters. Dana Heller suggests that *Anywhere but Here* supports Chodorow's analysis in *The Reproduction of Mothering:* "As long as there remains a capitalist industrial system founded on a firm division between the sexes, the spaces that men and women occupy, it is likely that women will remain the primary source of mothering. Consequently, their daughters are likely to reproduce the split in gender identification and continue operating predominantly in a relational mode based on maternal-filial sameness."[4] Identification may indeed be the issue, but Simpson structures the novel around a comic irony: Adele drives west to break free from life as defined by men, but Ann finally travels east when she realizes that her primary need is to escape not males but mothers. *Anywhere but Here* shows that the mother-daughter bond is often restrictive to the point of being negative.

Succinctly describing a general problem facing women who would rewrite the quest, Heller observes, "To seek out this territory and challenge the exclusive boundaries of gendered images and actions is to redefine heroism in terms specific to woman's experience in patriarchal culture" (105). Marilynne Robinson's celebration of female adventure has become a primary structure for novels of female bonding. Unlike Heller, however, who reads the meeting of transience and quest as women's liberation from "male-defined spaces," I suggest that the canonical paradigm of lighting out for the territory is itself a space determined by males which female writers do not escape but enter in order to revise from inside the form (106). The use of spatial metaphors to illustrate the quest has been at the heart of American fiction for nearly two hundred years, and contemporary female novelists are very much aware of the cultural changes to be wrought by varying the formula. Huck, for example, runs from his ostensible mothers, the Widow Douglas and Miss Watson, before finding his spiritual father on the great brown river. Similarly, Adele drives away from her own mother, Ida, but, unlike Huck, she initiates the quest in order to complete the self. To do so she must take Ann with her, only to watch as the bonded companion eventually rejects her. Ann abandons mother to develop selfhood, just as Adele deserts family to head west. Simpson exposes the danger of absorption in the mother-daughter bond.

Deborah Denenholz Morse reads Adele much less sympathetically than Heller does.[5] Describing Adele as "psychologically abusive," Morse finds the intensity of Adele's tie to Ann too "devouring" (67, 72). Heller treats as mere eccentricities Adele's manipulation of the supposedly masculine qualities of dominance and power, but Adele's erratic behavior lacks Sylvie's generosity. Never threatening Ruth, Sylvie helps her bonded friend turn her back on housekeeping. Adele, on the other hand, attempts to live both Ann's life for her and her own life through Ann. Sensing—but never pinpointing—an emptiness at the core of her experience because she is her mother's second daughter, Adele tries and fails to plug the gap by shaping her own daughter to her own needs. Daughters watch mothers and learn that selfhood is not a biological given but, instead, an earned state; thus, Ann breaks the bond by first telling her mother's story as a variation of the American paradigm and then walking out of the novel to begin writing her own tale. She illustrates her potential for negating the tie when she easily coerces friends into posing for nude photographs. Such coercion affirms that she can wield power rather than merely be its victim in her mother's hands. One might argue that Simpson's unexpected strategy of permitting Adele to narrate the last few pages reasserts the primacy of the bond, but Adele's final narration exposes her failure to accept Ann's insistence on selfhood as superior to Adele's desire for relationship. As Heller comments, "The appropriating gaze of the mother that refuses to recognize the child's separateness illustrates the 'psychotic distortion of the normal pre-oedipal relationship,' which

Chodorow identifies as predominantly a mother-daughter phenomenon" (108).

This is why Simpson writes Ann's voice to dominate the novel. By telling her own adventure, Ann simultaneously asserts the importance of the female voice and steps beyond the mother's reading of the text. Adele's commitment to cars and the wandering she associates with them indicates her repudiation of the cultural equation of female and home, her instinct to assume the freedom traditionally accorded male autonomy, and her affinity with the bonded males in *On the Road*. Although Ann longs for a home in the sense that Ruth and Sylvie do not, she learns from Adele's love of cars that houses are always read as both woman's space and woman's place, sites of permanence designed to keep women at home in order to liberate men to the transience of the quest in the wilderness. In other words, Adele shows Ann how to reject housekeeping, but to do so Ann must also resist mother. Ann's means of asserting self while holding onto family, as Leatherstocking and Huck never do, is to write her own life and give other mothers voices in the tale.

Ann announces the fragility of the bond with the first two words of the novel: "We fought" (3). Establishing tension between the need of family ("we") and the desire to break away ("fought"), Simpson creates a motif of abandonment in terms of both plot and theme: Adele periodically forces Ann from the car and drives off without her. The mother attempts to coerce the daughter to abandon her own life for the sake of the mother's dreams. Not yet a teenager, Ann senses the enormity of the adventure as the mother takes the daughter to California so that the latter may become a television star: "We were running away from family. We'd left home" (3). Home, Ann learns, "could have been anywhere" (6).

Ann's voice, usually frustrated, often sardonic, shapes the disparate parts of the quest, but, with Adele, Simpson creates a female character worthy of joining the rogues gallery of American fiction. Telling white lies with Huck, pulling off small swindles with the Confidence Man, relying on melodrama with Holden Caulfield—all three of whom have hit the road and crossed into the wilderness—Adele outrageously charms and steals her way toward the American Dream. Leatherstocking wants to escape the sound of the axes. Adele wants someone to pay the bills. Canonical American literature normally fails to accommodate such women. Despite Ann's frustration at being forced to endure the bond while still a child, Simpson suggests a kind of mysticism in the mother-daughter relationship so long as the former acknowledges the latter as a separate self. Such acknowledgment is rare in *Anywhere but Here*. When it does occur Simpson resorts to abstractions as Ann speaks of "some romance, some power" to account for women's strength: "And when she dies, the world will be flat, too simple, reasonable, too fair" (17).

Simpson's irony is that Adele simultaneously rejects men from the bond and pursues the romance of the quest to "catch" a father for Ann. In Simpson's revision of the paradigm Adele is the female adventurer who misreads the text. She tells Ann, for example, that Rhett Butler returns to Scarlett at the conclusion of *Gone with the Wind* because that is the way novels should end. Although she is on the road, she has not completely broken with the traditional canon, which writes women's closure as marriage or death. Bonding to Ann, stealing food, overextending credit cards in her dash across the continent, Adele nevertheless believes that disruption of home means dissolution of family. Guilt and insecurity mix with sexual desire in her unsuccessful efforts to snare a man. Speaking from hindsight, since *Anywhere but Here* is largely a flashback, Ann shrewdly penetrates to the center of her mother's compulsion to guarantee the bond: "it was one of the things she liked about having a daughter. You never were all alone" (31). With this one statement Simpson queries psychoanalytic theories that posit many female relationships on a preoedipal instinct to recreate mothering. Adele may be committed to Ann, but the force structuring the bond is fear of loneliness.

Revising the traditional American novel, Simpson rewrites *On the Road* without Kerouac's mythic search for the father. Mothers head west with daughters, while fathers and sons stay behind in a haven of matriarchy. Such a reversal of the canon might seem too neat, too much a political convenience designed to make a point about gender, except that Simpson features the daughter's desire to break the bond. Admitting that mothers initiate daughters into experience, Ann nevertheless says early in the novel: "You grow up and you leave them. She only had me six more years" (36). In the world of *Anywhere but Here* female bonding inhibits self.

This is why Simpson parodies Adele's housekeeping. Unlike Marilynne Robinson, who uses the conventional spick-and-span home as a metaphor of women's dormant lives, Simpson suggests that the ordered house is a misguided means of coercion by females. Adele's refusal to buy furniture, even though she indulges in obsessive binges of cleaning, illustrates her reluctance to adapt to the standard woman's role of homemaker, and thus she seems a distant cousin of Robinson's Sylvie. But the more important point is that Simpson develops house-

keeping to expose the negative side of female bonding. Women resort
to power just as readily as men. Adele uses both physical strength and
transparent lies to keep Ann tied to her:

> I started walking and her nails bit into my arm.
> "Oh, no you don't. You're not going anywhere. You're going to stay
> right here and clean, for a change. . . . I work all week while you're
> playing."
> "I go to school," I said.
>
> (47)

Rather than teach her daughter to hunt, fish, and throw or, for that
matter, to paint, sew, and sing, Adele forces Ann to vacuum each
square of the floor five times. One need not stress that Sam Fathers
raises Ike McCaslin differently. Adele's reproduction of mothering
means absorption of the bonded Other, but Ann's notion of selfhood
requires assertion of inividuality: "I thought of the years in front of
me when I would still need a mother. . . . I looked back once and
decided, I'm not going to do this. I left the vacuum cleaner going so
she'd still hear the noise and I ran outside" (49). Ann undertands that
something "had gone wrong" with Adele, that they should not have
to leave home, that they should have been girls together who stayed
out on the porch at night listening to trucks barreling down the high-
way, but she also knows that her mother's idea of relationship is gratification of self: "My mother said absolutely anything to me. It was as
if she were alone" (61, 68).

Marilynne Robinson describes Ruth and Sylvie in a reciprocal
relationship as Ruth grows away from her sister toward her surrogate
mother. Simpson, however, offers the unexpected variation that the
adolescent girl is wiser than the questing parent. For all her charm
and education Adele is the American adventurer who crosses into the
territory without being satisfied with either home or quest. Her world
is the elegance of illusion, stolen cars and credit. Not yet a teenager
and thus unable to dissolve the bond, Ann at age twelve informs the
reader of her inevitable rejection of Adele's fantasies: "I didn't want
a thing" (101). In *Anywhere but Here* solidification of self means separation from mother.

Adele's own mother does not understand such tensions. A woman
of an earlier generation, she is the female who stays home and who
continues to define gender according to the requirements of the canonical American text. Girls have babies; boys quest: "I suppose when
you have daughters, you end up with the families. I think when you
have boys, they go off and make a start by themselves, but your

daughters always come back to you. They bring their children home" (160). Adele, of course, does no such thing, and thus Simpson dramatizes the paradox of the female who assumes the male role but who cannot stop mothering. In her misguided notion of bonding Adele insists on leaving home so long as Ann does not leave her. Undercutting such utopian schemes as immediate revision of gender constructs, Simpson suggests with the portraits of grandmother, mother, and daughter the slow though inevitable rewriting of the text that will close not with Adele but with Ann.

Simpson poses Adele as a woman who rarely questions long-honored standards of gender. Despite her radical transformation to freedom on the road, Adele invariably judges acquaintances according to whether their actions are appropriate for men or women. She walks out of the novel of marriage and home by insinuating herself into the male adventure plot, but she also looks for traditional male protection. Adele is Simpson's portrait of the questing woman in the prefeminist moment of the early 1960s, the female who repudiates housekeeping but who longs to be conventionally feminine: "I just have to meet the man and catch him" (234). In Adele's reading of domestic life in America such women as her mother and sister stay home, while husbands and fathers go to work, have fun, desert family, act like boors, or die. Their absence is a continuing presence because Adele's need of independence leaves a gap. The result is that the daughter must resort to imagination to reconstruct the father's leaving, even though his desertion deconstructs the predictable female life of school, marriage, family, death. To close the gap the mother manipulates the bonding process: "Oh, Honey, you didn't even know your dad. You were too young to really know him. How could you miss him? . . . When people ask you that, you just say, No, not really, I'm very close to my mom" (211). Ann matures into female relationships unfortunately believing that men are people who have "nothing to do with me" (232).

In Simpson's account of female bonding the daughter distrusts the mother's promises but still believes her threats (251). Their bond is as imperfect as Natty Bumppo's and Chingachgook's is inviolate because one member treats the other as an object to be created, shaped, and possessed. Indeed, Adele examines Ann's body "with the full pride of possession," and, when she pulls down Ann's pants or asks Ann to disrobe in front of friends, Simpson suggests, the mother dominates the daughter sexually just as females accuse males of doing (344). The issue is power, a lesson that Ann learns by watching Adele. The negative fallout is the equation of sex and coercion. Detailing

Ann's first physical experience with a male, for example, Simpson shows the daughter assuming the "superior" position and then—unexpectedly—blending the frenzy of sex with a fantasy of murder. Astride the boy, Ann thinks, "It would be so easy to kill another person. . . . You'd just reach down" (406–7). Mothers love daughters but fail the bond because they cannot encourage separateness. To do so would be to concede incompleteness. Thus, Adele rewrites the past, reinvents her life, and blames the daughter for the mother's dreams.

Ann's lunge toward selfhood, toward a daughter's independence from a mother's myth, begins in earnest when she describes Adele's threat of "me or nothing": Adele is "stunned that I would choose nothing" (418). Even Adele's therapist, whom Simpson names Hawthorne to remind the reader of the connection to canonical American literature, tells Ann that her companion "sees what she wants to see" (431). With imagination and confidence in her ability to revise the paradigm Simpson reverses the momentum of the male journey westward and sends Ann back east to sever the bond by escaping the mother's plot. Reproduction of mothering encourages repression of self. Ann's determination is worthy of Huck Finn's: "I left lightly. . . . Anything to get away. . . . For years, I didn't go home. . . . That's what kids do, they leave" (448–49, 502).

Committed to the freedom of the road rather than the immobility of home, Adele remains Simpson's American dreamer, even to the extreme of putting the white Lincoln on cinder blocks to wait for Ann's return. But in Simpson's adaptation of the paradigm the bonded companions do not "go to hell" for one another. Rather, they are reconciled only when their separation becomes formal. Not until the conclusion of *Anywhere but Here* does Simpson reveal Adele's voice, knowing that the mother's point of view will be read ironically because it is tagged onto the daughter's story. Adele, for example, muses that mothering defines her—"It's the most important, beautiful, fulfilling thing I've ever done in my life, being a mother"—but the reader sees that Adele's need to possess Ann has warped their relationship (529). Mythologizing her life as the realist Huck never does, Adele fails to read the paradox that her quest for freedom imprisons Ann: "They tried—to make me and more than that, my child, into their mold. I had to let myself and my daughter go free. And mold in another way" (531). One finally admires Adele's commitment to life, to tomorrow and dreams, her willingness to play both father and mother to a daughter who will only break away; but one also understands Simpson's criticism of a female bond in which self absorbs Other. Given the last word in the novel, Adele insists on the selfish myth of Pygmalion: "I

made that beautiful girl" (534). Reproduction of mothering means
rejection of the Other's self.

Hilma Wolitzer: *Hearts*

Patriarchy is neutralized in the sixth week of marriage and on the
first page of Hilma Wolitzer's *Hearts* (1980).[6] Twenty-six years old and
barely able to drive, Linda Reismann loses her new husband to a heart
attack a dozen lines into the novel. Stuck with a sullen teenaged
stepdaughter named Robin, Linda drives west, away from New Jersey,
to deposit the young woman with relatives before pursuing her own
quest in what she assumes is the promised land of California. As naive
as Huck Finn, and as brave, Linda is a walking thesaurus of clichés
and codes, a person whose every description and dream seem to come
straight from the pablum of network television or the advice columns
of popular magazines.

That Wolitzer deliberately sets out to revise the American canon
by making women the focus of a trek across the continent is clear from
the moment Linda learns to drive, but *Hearts* is not a mirror image of
Anywhere but Here. Simpson's novel charts the progressive deterioration
of a female bond that is forged by necessity and broken by need.
Adele and Ann begin with relationship but end with separation. *Hearts*,
on the other hand, uses the spatial metaphor of the quest to indicate
the distance women have to travel to meet one another. Linda and
Robin start with separation but conclude with the possibility of bonding. Robin's last words are "We're here!"—the only time in the novel
she is generous enough to include Linda in the "we" (247).

The end of *Hearts* does not suggest, however, that Wolitzer takes
a serene view of mutual distrust among women. Despite her prevailing
comic tone, a mode that she controls masterfully, she faces the political
issues of gender. Elizabeth Pochoda reads Linda as a modern exemplum when contrasted with Isabel Archer: "Neither rich nor beautiful,
imaginative nor presumptuous, she cannot even be said to do battle
with her destiny since it is the peculiar burden of contemporary women
like Linda, rootless and unhurried in the progress through life, to
appear to have a multitude of somewhat unclear destinies from which
to choose."[7] Pochoda's Linda is larger than mine. With the male dead
on the first page and thus permanently eliminated from the bond,
Linda confronts choices that define the complications of mothering.
Confined in a car with a surly stepdaughter when she herself has hardly
been a wife, Linda must discover simultaneously how to be both a
mother and a self. That she must also learn to drive as a preliminary

to the quest is a comic perplexity, which Wolitzer develops with gusto to dismantle the male certainty of such canonical plunges into the wilderness as *On the Road*. Linda can either mother Robin or abandon her. She thinks she chooses the middle course by heading away from the familiar congestion of northern New Jersey to leave the girl with her deceased husband's relatives, who live in what she imagines are the pastoral wilds of Iowa. Anything west of Jersey is the territory to Linda, the apparent domain of heroic males, and thus Wolitzer begins *Hearts* with a description of a map just as James Dickey does in *Deliverance*.

But Wolitzer adds the irony that Linda is unexpectedly pregnant. The complexities of mothering her husband's daughter are multiplied by the prospect of mothering her own. If canonical male novelists repel females from the journey down the river, or on the ocean, or through the forest, they at least speculate about what might happen if women were to cross the border. Children, especially daughters, are never an issue, except perhaps in such novels as *The Prairie* (1827), but Ishmael Bush's offspring are already grown. Female writers of the 1980s, however, bring both women and children to the quest, and in doing so they appropriate the venerable paradigm in ways that Cooper, Hemingway, and Dickey would never have imagined. Sensitive to the recent politicization of gender, Wolitzer details not psychoanalytic theories of preoedipal bonding or sentimental notions about the sanctity of family but, rather, the first question of mothering itself: whether to have the baby. This query engages another, for in part of *Hearts* Wolitzer expands the issue of female relationship beyond two women on the road to include all women and their wombs. Unable to bond with Robin for most of the journey, much less reproduce mothering, Linda decides to abort the fetus. The scene of the violent protest at the abortion clinic explodes such political fantasies as female solidarity and women agreeing on the matter of controlling their own bodies: "Linda stared at them [policemen] and had her first conscious feminist thought. This was a civil war, women against women, and the policemen were out of it, non-partisan, merely keepers of the law" (88). Wolitzer develops the conflict between Linda and Robin as a metaphor of "women against women." Watching groups of females on opposite sides of a barricade scream at each other over the intricacies of abortion, Robin thinks, "The world was full of assorted lunacy and sorrow, most of it readied for instant publicity" (110).

Wolitzer shows that so-called women's questions are personal issues having more to do with individuality than gender. Deftly satirizing both the traditional view of motherhood and the politics of feminism, she places Linda in the midst of a contemporary dilemma in which women turn on women, much as Robin turns on Linda, and thereby violate a person's privacy: "She hoped the pickets would be gone when she got there this time, away on a coffee break or something. It was a private matter, strictly a personal decision, and they were turning it into some kind of public extravaganza" (102).

The dismissal of the male is more problematical. Wolitzer frames *Hearts* so that the death of the husband at the beginning balances the rejection of the lover at the end. No male is acceptable when females try to bond, a narrative device in contemporary novels by women which paradoxically reverses the traditional American novel of the masculine quest *(The Last of the Mohicans)* and counters the recent American novel written by men, which revises the paradigm to include women *(A Prayer for Owen Meany)*. Even the lover's name expresses the intensity of the issue—Wolitzer calls him Wolfe to indicate male aggression. When Linda dismisses him with the news that she plans to have the baby, she acts out a general thesis of feminist anthropology which argues that women choose from among authoritative males rather than wait to be chosen.[8] Thus, one assumes, Linda learns that she need not be dependent on traditional male protection.

Yet the lesson seems extreme. Robin's presence complicates this particular dilemma of gender relationships, a dilemma that has been debated in American culture since the 1960s, because Robin is always sullen and usually unsympathetic. She communicates in grunts. She rebuffs Linda's expressions of concern. She takes for granted Linda's sacrifice for her. She gobbles junk food. She carries drugs. She is, in short, no homeless Huck Finn or bewildered Holden Caulfield or wandering Augie March—and she is surely no Lolita. One anonymous commentator describes her as "among the most horrid little girls in recent memory." That Robin's adolescent petulance is occasionally comic is secondary to the more relevant question of whether males must always be repudiated for the sake of female bonding, even when one of the women is disagreeable. The same anonymous reviewer makes the point: "That Linda decides to go her own way, with her miserable ward at her side instead of a man, testifies to an emergent sense of self-purpose and self-creation. But it also rings of the new sentimentality of the new women's fiction—that happiness might lie just around the corner, if only a woman remains strong enough to go it alone."[9] How far, in other words, must female novelists go to revise a literature that traditionally imagines female characters as either married or dead? The recent emphasis by women on gender exclusivity is unusual when one considers that it is being urged by the very people who were once written out of the text of male advanture.

Yet comedy keeps *Hearts* from degenerating into polemics. Before embarking on the journey, for example, Linda must consult a map of the territory beyond New Jersey, and thus Wolitzer indirectly parodies the American literary hero who knows where to go without determining how to get there. Even more important, Linda is no mythic explorer of rivers and forests, no larger-than-life quester striding across the horizon in pursuit of immortality. Wolitzer describes her as "ordinary in a frightening, anonymous way," and the comedy counters the psychology of woman's victimization which Diane Johnson investigates in *The Shadow Knows* when N. suspects that she is about to be murdered. Wolitzer undercuts the dramatic effect of such fears: "Linda believed she was going to be killed. Unidentified body of young woman between the ages of. . . . Mutilated beyond. . . . Dental charts necessary for. . . . She realized that she had not been to a dentist for over two years. Instead of being murdered, she ended up getting married" (29, 30–31).

When the husband's death initiates the long drive westward Wolitzer parodies the masculine text of life on the road—or on the raft, the trail, and the ocean—by creating a heroine who can hardly drive. Linda is such an inexperienced quester that she does not recognize obscenity in the gestures of drivers frustrated at her bungling: "Was she supposed to return them as part of some unwritten code of the road?" (2). Sal Paradise would be appalled. So is Robin. Brash where Linda is meek, Robin dubs the ostensible leader of the bond "Linda the Wimp." More to the point than the joke, however, is that Wolitzer reverses entrenched tales of the cruel stepmother, myths created primarily by men. In her revision the stepdaughter meets the stepmother's generosity with boorishness: "Linda lay back on hers and massaged her hands. They were still curled from steering, and looked like the hands of Snow White's stepmother when she was cackling over the poisoned apple. In the other bed, Snow White herself lay, pale and bored" (44).

Elimination of husbands and fathers propels Linda into what the narrator calls "traffic and the world" (12). Unaware that the American need to pull up stakes and take to the road is not a migratory instinct but a cultural myth, she assumes that the goal is to reestablish roots rather than reaffirm self. This is why she idealizes her plan of finding Robin a new family with relatives in the Midwest. Not yet free of the masculine text, she accepts the equation of female and home. Contrary to the requirements of the male quest in American fiction, Wolitzer shows that missing mothers, not absent fathers, are the issue. Huck Finn and Ike McCaslin find spiritual paternity in Jim and Sam Fathers, and Sal Paradise and Dean Moriarty crisscross a continent in pursuit of the latter's father, but the adolescent heroines in the novels of Marilynne Robinson, Mona Simpson, and Hilma Wolitzer search for mothers. This does not mean that American female writers of the 1980s sentimentalize motherhood. Ruth's mother kills herself *(House-keeping)*, and Ann's mother stifles her *(Anywhere but Here)*. In *Hearts* Wolitzer indirectly questions Nancy Chodorow's thesis about the reproduction of mothering when the narrator reveals that Robin's mother had deserted her after the child's fifth birthday. Preoedipal instincts that enhance mothering are beside the point. Just as Linda must struggle to become a mother, so Robin must learn to act the daughter. The process is difficult because, as Wolitzer and her peers argue, female relationships are often tenuous and occasionally nonexistent.

The American literary canon has taught that males bond before crossing the border to the territory of adventure: in *The Last of the Mohicans; Moby-Dick; Huckleberry Finn; Go Down, Moses; On the Road;* and *Deliverance;* among others. Wolitzer's revision suggests, on the other hand, that the difficulty of bonding defines the female quest novel. Ironically linked together in the interior of a car, Linda and Robin are nevertheless separate when they leave New Jersey. And more: unlike Dickey's veneration of the wild river or Faulkner's glorification of the big woods or Melville's appreciation of the endless ocean, Wolitzer does not romanticize the wilderness as if most of the United States were a painting by the Hudson River school. Her account of American vastness recalls not Cooper's grandeur but Nabokov's parody: glitzy motels, bright lights, disgusting food. As a mechanic says to Linda when she explains the adventure as an opportunity to see America: "Yeah, well don't be disappointed. An awful lot of it looks like Jersey" (33). Comic deflation of the paradigm could not be sharper.

Neither could Wolitzer's joke that the eliminated male tags along in the guise of his own ashes. Stored in a small box in the trunk of the car, the remains of the husband-father witness, as it were, the discovery of the mother. Robin believes that society prefers male children, and thus her pursuit of the mother reflects the search for self. Linda's pregnancy is the other side of Robin's need, for the one finds mothering, while the other finds a mother. Yet neither of them realizes until the end of the novel that their failed bond hinders fulfillment of self, which, in *Hearts*, means women without men, the very reversal of Hemingway's famous adage. In Robin's imaginary narrative of locating the missing parent the daughter avenges the father's ashes by punishing the deserting mother. Revising her memories, Robin rewrites tales of romance traditionally associated with female authors:

> Gradually, since her father's death, her mind's image of her mother changed, too. The beauty she believed she remembered became shallow and ordinary. . . . Her mother would cry out in grief and lay apologies like roses at Robin's feet, too late, too late. Then joy would overtake her at rediscovering her lost child and she would open her arms. Robin would go into them, but only to exact her revenge. (48)

In the drive to find the self, mother becomes Other. Linda, too, longs for mothering once she realizes the unfairness of female biology in the connection between sex and procreation. Pregnant and stuck with a surrogate daughter who already treats her as Other, she must redefine male notions of heroism to fit the female adventure. The ashes in the back of the car signal the uselessness of masculine heroics in the 1980s.

To complete the redefinition Linda reassesses her understanding of women. Wolitzer satirizes contemporary feminist theories of solidarity as readily as she exposes fallacies of male bonding. Linda naively believes, for instance, that women share some kind of mystical relationship: "Although she and Sally had not had an intimate friendship in high school, there was a natural intimacy among all women these days" (68). Such is not the case, as Wolitzer humorously documents. Her point is that individuals, not genders, bond. The process is not idyllic, and it normally does not occur prior to the quest. Wolitzer's account of the Tupperware party is an ironic gem designed to illustrate female chicanery. Hawking plastic sex gadgets, the saleswoman suckers the housewives by equating women's freedom with erotic fantasy. Note how she distances herself from what she denigrates as "libbers":

> I'm really proud to be a woman, too, an *American* woman, who is modern enough to want to make my marriage an exciting and lasting relationship. Things have changed since our mother's and grandmother's day. Women are equal with men in many ways. . . . Don't get me wrong; I'm no libber, but I am for equal rights, for freedom of choice in *certain* areas of life. (74–75)

The certain area is, of course, sex, and Linda discovers that "natural intimacy" among women is a bogus idea designed to empower someone else.

If Linda learns anything on her journey through the wilderness, it is that she must write her own tale. The problem is that women's lives are often determined by women's stories, which are usually defined by men. Linda understands that sentimental conclusions to novels designed to deal with "real" issues are false applications of literature to life and that her sense of the orderliness of nature is an illusion generated by her memory of *Heidi,* but she does not know how to substitute the text: "There was much human cruelty in the story [*Heidi*], the way there was in life, but goodness and justice had triumphed in the end" (80). Such a narrative implies closure, which Wolitzer denies. To escape the canon Linda must create her own story by living it.

She has a hard time doing so. Not until she abandons the hope that her dead husband's father is the person with whom to deposit Robin can she determine a legitimate reason for the adventure. Linda and Robin take the first tentative step toward bonding when they agree to journey toward the latter's mother in the far west. Robin looks at her navel and thinks: "You were once attached to your mother there. If the cord was never cut and tied, you could not be lost from one another" (93). Linda recalls similar fears from her own childhood. But the cord is cut, and they are lost, as Wolitzer documents at the end, when Robin's mother bungles the reunion. In *Hearts* mothering is neither a biological given nor a necessary instinct. Bonding is an artificial construct to be created. Unlike the male novels of the paradigm, *Hearts* traces a quest that ends, but does not close, with the beginning of a possible bond. The question of a relationship's continuity is material for a different novel: "The mystery of love's beginning was nothing compared to the miracle of its endurance" (152).

In a narrative in which no male is reliable and most are threats, which is common in women's fiction in the 1980s, Wolfe's sexual lure represents a final hurdle to commitment. When Linda turns to Wolfe during the festivities of another couple's marriage, Wolitzer shows that women are trained to look to men as protectors of wives and children. But to conclude *Hearts* with Wolfe and Linda is to revisit rather than revise the tradition: attractive male marries spunky woman, adopts surrogate daughter, and raises unwanted baby. Wolitzer chooses the other extreme and banishes men altogether. Her comic irony is that Robin watches Wolfe and Linda, then reads a sentimental conclusion taken from conventional women's stories: "They were like characters she had been cheering on in a movie, for whom she wanted a satisfying ending, and they were also heroes in her real life" (208). Linda teaches her to reread the text, to understand that the new heroes are not Wolfe and Linda but, rather, Robin and Linda. Together they adapt the canon to their own story: "crossing that border into being was such a daring act" (223).

Indeed it is. Wolitzer celebrates the reinventing of women's lives when the two females finally scatter the ashes of the husband-father in a distant forest. She uses the word *bound* to describe their relationship at the end of *Hearts*, and one realizes that the imperfection of the bond indicates not a sentimental but a genuine addition to the text. Yet an unanswered question remains: Are women without men the reverse of a discredited cultural myth? Does politics determine art?

Meg Wolitzer: *This Is Your Life*

Early in Meg Wolitzer's *This Is Your Life* (1988) the narrator describes Dottie Engels's appearance on the "Johnny Carson Show":[10] "Sitting between Johnny and Ed, with the skyline tableau stretched out behind her, she gestured broadly and flooded the entire screen. In that moment the men disappeared, were swallowed up, and even the skyline was eclipsed" (7). Diminishment of the male is a given in *This Is Your Life*, as fat, garrulous, funny Dottie utterly dwarfs men, all but reduces them to nonentities. In the mind of her young daughter she personifies a "huge and luminous" moon, an "explosion" (7). Various commentators describe Dottie as a cross between Erma Bombeck and Joan Rivers, Totie Fields and Joan Rivers, and Phyllis Diller and Joan Rivers—but the more important issue is that Dottie works as a single parent of two children: small, pretty Opal and fat, defensive Erica.[11] The mother-daughter bond is unusual in *This Is Your Life* because the mother is nearly always absent, playing to audiences in California or Las Vegas, present to the daughters primarily via televised image or telephone voice. That Meg Wolitzer is Hilma Wolitzer's daughter suggests the special tension involved in a mother-daughter relationship when the parent is public and famous.

Yet, for all the larger-than-life presence of Dottie's absence, Wolitzer develops her novel to trace the gradual disintegration of the sibling bond. So long as the sisters are young enough to be confined to apartment and school they seem united for life. Wolitzer comically makes the point in the first two sentences of the novel: "It was her sister who taught her how to hyperventilate. They sat facing each other on the bed, and they panted together like husband and wife in a Lamaze workshop" (3). Together they are Wolitzer's parody of the anthropological thesis that locates the origin of human society with the development of male hunting. Primarily an opinion of biological determinism, the notion of man-the-hunter posits men bonding together to protect the group and to provide food while women gather grain and raise offspring.[12] Fat Dottie's journey west to the hunting grounds of show biz is Wolitzer's laugh at such anthropologists as Lionel Tiger,[13] but her most slashing riposte involves the daughters. With the mother in California, which the girls imagine as a "remote" wilderness, the females left behind do not harvest grain but "hunt for supper" (8, 5).

Revising the canon by rewriting the quest, Wolitzer joins other female novelists of the 1980s to show that, contrary to the fiction of Cooper and Twain, women no longer personify the stable, the inert, the parlor, the kitchen, the home. Nor do they serve as icons of eroticism for the male text. Neither pretty nor thin, Dottie is huge and "wonderful" (9). Her forays into the territory force a society trained to male definitions of beauty to acknowledge the fat and, thus, to respond not to her looks but to her. With Dottie away on the hunt Opal reads to learn how to write her own life, but she peruses books with such titles as *New Girl at Adams High* in which the actions of boys define the happiness of girls. Dottie is the new text.

Wolitzer apparently agrees with her peers that revitalization of the tradition requires removal of the male. The daughters' absent father, for example, supplies the family name but is remembered as its "weakest link." Appearing only at dinner and for arguments, he finally disappears for good, leaving the women behind with a name that they live with like "the child of someone who has left you and whom you now despise" (14). In a traditional American novel the female might tend the home fires while waiting for the adventuring male to wander his way back to the family. Penelope weaves while Ulysses quests. But in *This Is Your Life* the bonded women rejoice at the father's absence, equating his presence with incarceration: "a father who paced the hall like a warden, clearly uneasy in that house of females. He expected treachery from them, abandonment, and finally he got both" (24).

The new standard of gender exclusivity might overwhelm fiction with polemic were it not for laughter. *Housekeeping, Anywhere but Here, Hearts,* and *This Is Your Life* feature a prevailing tone of comedy. The reader smiles as the novelist throws the barb, always aware, however, that the politics of gender shapes the center. This is why Wolitzer stresses the humor of the daughters' school play. Preadolescent girls are rehearsed to act out T. S. Eliot's "The Hollow Men," and one laughs when they intone lines that Eliot meant to be generic but which Wolitzer makes gender specific: "We are the stuffed men, leaning together. Headpiece filled with straw" (27). Reading the text, the females remember the father. To them he is the true Hollow Man because, as the embodiment of patriarchy, he has *"access* to their lives" (31). The female journey begins when the male is abandoned. As the mother says to the daughters when they literally drive away from the father, "Think of it as an adventure" (33). Even as a girl, Opal understands, after peering into her male cousin's bedroom, that men collect athletics trophies, pin maps of the world to the wall, and go forth. Wolitzer uses the word *extricated* with regard to the father left behind to indicate an active rather than a passive distancing from masculinity. The woman does not wait to be chosen by the man; rather, she deliberately repudiates his authority. Opal and Erica bond only through childhood, but so long as they stick together they can exclude a father who accuses them of being cold and who predicts their maturation into "frigid" women (38). He is wrong, of course, as the young girls finally realize, but he illustrates the masculine determination to evaluate femininity according to erotic intensity.

Wolitzer revises the standard definition of the nuclear family—male, female, two children—to read female and two children. Only *un*happy families, Opal learns, take to the road to pursue togetherness in some far-flung vacation spot. This is why Dottie makes a living by telling whoppers about life with father and husband. Audiences laugh at her self-deprecation, but the male is part of the joke. Erica's memory of fathers as only people to do the driving expresses Wolitzer's dismissal of the classic American tale of males bonding together on the road. In *This Is Your Life* the patriarch is missing, threatening, or silent. Gender exclusivity is clear: "It had been a long time since Erica had been around anybody's father for more than a few minutes. She had forgotten the dynamic, the way you were supposed to act, but soon it came back to her: shy deference, with underpinnings of respect and fear" (90). Men are no more than "shadow puppet[s]" who protect not females, as is traditionally assumed, but maleness (96).

The bond between the daughters holds so long as they commit to the adventuring mother, but Erica's turn toward her drug-addicted boyfriend precipitates the strain. More militant in her portrayal of gender relations than Marilynne Robinson or Mona Simpson, Wolitzer all but blames women for using men to break the bond. By characterizing Erica as fat and homely, she asks a significant question: What happens to a female who does not respond to male definitions of culture? Male confidence exacerbates female inferiority. Wolitzer strikes hard when, early in the novel, she associates Erica's boyfriend, Jordan, with the anthropological thesis of man-the-hunter:

> Jordan was obsessed with paperbacks from the Sixties; Hunter Thompson
> was his hero. He referred to him continually as "Hunter." . . . Jordan
> had given Erica a copy of *Fear and Loathing in Las Vegas*, and she had
> stared blankly at it for hours, missing the point. It was all about messy,
> crazed men driving fast or taking hallucinogens. This side of the
> counterculture, or what was left of it in the 1970s, seemed to have been
> designed specifically for *boys*. (17)

The male canon defines American culture, and thus Erica cannot read
the text. Unlike the mother, who revises the tradition with laughter,
the daughter embraces the very narrative that excludes her. Her sense
of inadequacy is so extreme that she negates relationship with women
to solicit attention from men. In Wolitzer's characterization of gender,
attraction to males strains affinity among females. Opal watches Erica
drift toward Jordan and thinks of the bond: "It was like the slow
failing of a marriage. . . . maybe there was no such thing as extended
harmony" (23). A note of bitterness darkens the humor when Wolitzer
describes Erica as walking behind the man like a silent Japanese wife.

Erica's commitment to a male because of self-hatred is the most
negative criticism of gender relationships in the novels thus far discussed. Even when she is with Jordan, Erica realizes that she is not
part of any whole. Sex with a man does not compensate for a failed
bond with a woman. Opal is different. Expelled from her childhood
society of two, she learns that her slimness and beauty are socially
sanctioned entries to a culture in which successful females have blond
flips and wear short dresses. Erica's failure as a Junior Peace Corps
volunteer in Africa accelerates the disintegration of the bond with Opal
and illustrates the clear-eyed perspective that merely leaving family
and home does not turn an unhappy woman into a questing adventurer. Dramatizing a break in a relationship that has held firm since
girlhood, Wolitzer reaffirms the bond between Dottie and Opal—
mother and daughter—before pulling the rug from under reader and
characters: fickle audiences decide that Dottie is no longer funny.

Wolitzer's variation on Chodorow's thesis is a primary contribution
to contemporary fiction, for she suggests that the mother's success defines the daughter's identity. Aware of Dottie's fall from adulation, Opal
turns from sister to mother in order to protect the latter, but she soon
realizes that the mother's public persona absorbs the daughter's private
self: "She had been Dottie Engels's daughter; that was what she had
done best of all" (107). The reproduction of mothering does not necessarily encourage reciprocal relationships. The irony—and it is sharply
developed in *This Is Your Life*—is that feminism alters women's percep-
tions of gender to such an extreme that women are persuaded to reject a

Dottie Engels, who once encouraged females to laugh at themselves: "When I first started out, everyone said it was so wonderful how far I'd come, what a good role model I was for other women, and now they're saying that my humor is *insulting* to women" (109). Even more pungent is the following observation by a minor character: "I mean, look at how the women's movement changed everything. Suddenly everybody got a little embarrassed if women made jokes about their bodies" (154). Obsession with women's issues, these characters suggest, makes females too self-conscious, too defensive, too humorless.

Blaming the popular culprit, patriarchy, is a dodge of more unpleasant issues. Wolitzer does not hesitate to point out that women turn on women who ignore the model that society reserves for them, even in an age of so-called raised consciousness. With Dottie and Erica she develops similar characters who respond to body size in opposite ways. Rejected by the very women who once joined her in the laughter, Dottie takes the offensive by sponsoring colorful fashions for large females. Erica has a more difficult time. Repudiated by other women, she reacts defensively and withdraws behind the protection of her own obesity: "Erica was the kind of woman who was never sprayed with perfume in department stores. She would step off the escalator and watch as the grimly smiling models turned from her and aimed their atomizers elsewhere" (116). Rather than idealize relationships, as canonical male writers tend to do, Wolitzer concedes the flaws in the bond. The spurned woman takes the public rebuff as her cue and responds in turn by denying private ties to mother and sister.

The women in *This Is Your Life* have different longings, separate needs, and Wolitzer uses the disagreements to describe the failed bond ironically. Dottie's fashion commercials, for instance, attract Erica, the daughter who resists relationships, but they repulse Opal, the daughter who values bonding. Wolitzer frames the tension within the changing concept of family, a demographic phenomenon that has slowly reshaped American life since the 1960s. Admitting that "the desire to keep a family together seemed primitive," Opal nevertheless longs for the traditional unit that includes males, even while she believes that the mother's various lovers threaten ties to the daughter (130). Conversely, Dottie and Erica think nothing of drifting from home for extended periods, suggesting that shifting location combines with gender exclusivity in outlining new definitions of family. That Erica becomes a kind of housemother to a group of drug-addicted teenagers is the novel's sad joke about unstable bonding.

With an indirect allusion to Hilma Wolitzer's *Hearts,* a fiction in which the father dies from a coronary, Meg Wolitzer nudges the characters toward reconciliation when Dottie suffers a heart attack. Only then does Erica realize that Dottie's presence guarantees her own safety, that mothers protect daughters by being "*out* there," that is, out in the wilderness where, traditionally, women do not go (200). Arguing the necessity of the mother-daughter bond, Wolitzer describes women with dying mothers as the "disenfranchised, the alienated, the lost" (204–5). She rejects current clichés about gender, such as that males mistreat females because they do not appreciate "womanhood," and she investigates friction among women instead. The mother's collapse threatens not only the reproduction of mothering but also the affinity of sisters, and thus Erica wonders whether she should write a book with the revealing title *Women Who Hate Women*. To return home is not to reaffirm relationship before setting out once more on the quest, as is often the case in traditional American fiction, because the equation of home and family no longer holds. The strained bond between Erica and Opal is such that there is "nothing to mark them as sisters" (226). All they share are the external properties of a seriously ill mother and some fugitive bits of joint history. The long-honored staple of searching for the father to stabilize the family only antagonizes the bond, for in *This Is Your Life*, as in other novels by women in the 1980s, fathers either are absent or are present merely as voices on a long-distance wire.

One is not certain at the conclusion of *This Is Your Life* whether the renewal of bonding between mother and daughter is a sign of security or a promise of frustration. The sisters, after all, are reconciled only because of the mother's emergency, and her recovery and subsequent loss of weight are developed as both a comic resolution and a threat. At the end Wolitzer reminds the reader of the importance of the female journey, for Erica and Opal travel west to visit Dottie at a nursing home. Yet Wolitzer also suggests the fragility of the reestablished relationship when she describes the daughters' reaction to a suddenly thin and therefore obviously different mother. Dottie, in other words, produces a new self rather than reproduces mothering, and the alteration reintroduces uncertainty to the bond: "The change both astonished and frightened [Opal]; she felt as though her mother had not so much changed as disappeared" (262). Although the women breathe in synchrony while jogging at the edge of the sea, an allusion to Opal's childhood game of hyperventilating with Erica, Wolitzer does not arbitrarily deny friction to affirm solidarity. To do so would be to recall the sentimentality associated with women's fiction in the nineteenth century. Wolitzer is no sentimentalist. The female bond in *This Is Your Life* is as fragile as Dottie's heart.

Joan Chase: *During the Reign of the Queen of Persia*

The very title of Joan Chase's *During the Reign of the Queen of Persia* (1983) alerts readers to the power of matriarchy before they even turn to the first page.[14] Named the queen by a son-in-law, Gram asserts her authority as matriarch with the strength and coercion traditionally assigned to fathers in American fiction. The time is the 1950s, and Gram's farm in northern Ohio represents a wilderness of women, a self-contained territory where five daughters and four granddaughters gather, where life's cyclical patterns suggest a femininity opposed to male notions of linear progress, and where men are accepted as little more than nuisances. In this splendid first novel—as significant as *Housekeeping* yet all but unknown—Chase investigates the tenuousness of the female bond when women are empowered to compete among themselves.

Like *Housekeeping*, *During the Reign of the Queen of Persia* directly challenges the staples of the American canon. In her review of the novel Margaret Atwood illustrates how a shift of perspective encourages a change in fiction:

> "Lighting out for the territory" is a motif that has long been held to be central to the tradition of American fiction. When informed by it, a novel is about what happens when a single, usually male loner—call him Ishmael, or Huckleberry, or transpose him into a 20th-century mode, as in F. Scott Fitzgerald, E. L. Doctorow, Raymond Chandler and many more—breaks away from his matrix and has adventures. But elevate, say, Louisa May Alcott's "Little Women" to a more important position in the line of ancestral descent, and the perspective shifts. "Moby Dick" would have been quite different if written from the point of view of Ishmael's mother and sisters; in fact, it wouldn't have been "Moby Dick" at all, since, for them, Captain Ahab and whales and other images of Romanticism have no place except over the mantelpiece.[15]

Indeed, Gram's appropriation of the male quest is as firm as her rejection of men: she places a framed picture of a Native American above the mantel. Having symbolically truncated the male journey by trapping it in a house, she reduces to retainers the people who once strode across the border to create an American myth: husbands, sons, and assorted lovers.

Yet Chase offers no sunny celebration of female authority, no political pipe dream of women's independence. If the men resort to verbal abuse, isolation, and drink, the women share the blame. Gram's males may be failed questers, like gentle Uncle Dan, who abandons his dream of California for the sake of peace in Ohio, or they may be eccentric isolates, like Gram's husband, Grandad, who takes his violence to the barn to escape matriarchy in the house, but the tension between the sexes transcends mere verbal warfare. As Atwood observes, "The women appropriate moral self-righteousness and beat the men over the head with it, mercilessly, endlessly; the men react with sneers, escapes and, when nothing else is left for them, physical violence" (9). Ellen Sweet argues that women in *During the Reign of the Queen of Persia* "are bonded by their contempt for the men who fail them," but a more accurate reading illustrates how each gender fails the other.[16] Fran Schumer has a point: "it is a comment on life in this house full of women that Grandad prefers to spend his time in the company of his cows."[17]

Chase constructs the novel with a point of view that is unmistakably feminine but hardly feminist. Rather than reject the canon as male oriented and thus unsuited to women's needs, she adapts it. Not sisterhood but sisters are the focus. Tension between mother and daughter is as frequent as friction between husband and wife, and the result is a novel of generations which honors female adventure without idealizing female power.

To investigate the complexities of gender Chase develops an organic relationship between technique and theme. She designates female bonding through the first-person plural pronoun, and her astonishing use of *we* as the narrator expresses the uniformity of women's perspective despite the fragility of women's relationships. Chase's narrative technique is so successful that it earns Atwood's praise: "That the narrator is a 'we' rather than an 'I' is entirely fitting, for this book is about the power—by no means always positive—of the collective female consciousness" (9).[18] Literally, the "we" encompasses Gram's four granddaughters, who collectively roam the farm as if it were an Eden of endless female adventure, but, as the novel unfolds, the "we" metaphorically speaks for all women who have staked a claim to the territory. Using an inclusive narrative voice rather than the restrictive first or third person normally associated with novels of male bonding, Chase structures the episodes of *During the Reign of the Queen of Persia* as variations on a theme, as a fugue. In doing so she radically revises the linear plot that is a hallmark of the male quest. The processes of memory become an active force instead of a passive reflection, and the narrator-as-*we* superimposes events and dialogue to suggest the interconnection of the female experience. The question, unstated but never ignored, is whether the power of the "we" prevents the development of the "I." Is Gram's matriarchy, in other words, so coercive that the collection of women around her remains a satellite to her sun?

Like other significant novels by women in the 1980s, *During the Reign of the Queen of Persia* begins with the diminishment of the male. The chapters on Grandad and Neil, for example, document the marginalizing of masculine prerogatives by the release of feminine authority. More significant is the plight of Uncle Dan. Always gentle and occasionally musing, he has been sidetracked in his effort to walk the footsteps of Leatherstocking and Huck. Chase stresses at the outset the isolation of the farm, its sense of settlement on the edge of nowhere, where "traces of human habitation recede" (3). From the perspective of the collective narrator the farm is the focus of the world and, thus, a paradox when judged in terms of the American literary tradition: it is a periphery that seems a center, a wilderness that holds a civilization. Males bond to escape such impediments to the quest as kitchens and children, but in Chase's novel females both bond in the territory and sit with daughters by the stove. Thus, while Dan lives in the matriarchy, he is not of it. In a canonical novel of bonding such as *The Last of the Mohicans* the offending gender either dies within the wilderness (Cora) or retreats from it (Alice), but in *During the Reign of the Queen of Persia* the power of the female bond is more subtle. Dan is neither killed nor removed; he is first trapped and then ignored.

To make the point Chase initially characterizes Dan as a male adventurer, then denies him the plot. He has read the canonical text: he was a marine during World War II; he got as far west as California; he dreams of picking up the trail after the truce. But what is wilderness to the woman is stasis to the man, and the Ohio farm at the edge of "human habitation" neutralizes rather than nurtures him. Married to one of Gram's daughters, he counts the years, longs to begin his life again by going forth, and stays where he is. The collective female narrator senses his frustration but dismisses his need: "But when Uncle Dan talked to us about his job, his life, as though he too were secured with a chain, which, though invisible, bound as securely, we never worried" (7).

They do not worry because Gram, not Dan, is the pioneer. Contrary to the hypotheses of such anthropologists as Lionel Tiger, who stress the formative role of man-the-hunter, loss of the male would mean nothing in *During the Reign of the Queen of Persia*. Gram has revised the privileged status of Natty Bumppo, has staked out the territory, and has supplied the food. At a given moment Dan is the only man in a household of ten or more women who think of him only as "a surviving male figure" (11). When he advises the girls "to stick to known territory," he exposes his inability to reread the text that has shaped his sense of manhood (15). He longs to be a pathfinder, a hunter, a marine—an adventurer through the canon of American fiction—but Gram has rewritten the novel. She defines a world in the wilderness, and she slaps dinner on the table at five o'clock whether anyone is ready to eat or not. Chase's irony is sharp: Dan is the local butcher who has to hire someone else to do the killing. At the conclusion of the novel the "we" hears in his voice "the sound of endings, his life something that had happened a long time ago" (261).

But that is just Chase's point: the time of male deerslayers and pathfinders is long past. To reenter the canon would be to rebuff the female. Better to revise the text. The result, however, is reversed gender exclusivity in women's fiction of the 1980s. The man is either erased from the tale or relegated to the back pages at the very moment when contemporary male authors write women as the center of male bonding. Chase's innovation is that masculinity is not entirely at fault. Men are pushed to the periphery not because they are insensitive or coercive or physical but, rather, because women have assumed a stance of moral superiority which, they believe, authorizes them to repudiate all who disagree. Chase shows matriarchy to be not a neutralizing of aggression but merely the other side of patriarchy.

This does not mean that Gram and her daughters and granddaughters are always negative, evil, or small-minded. Early in the novel Chase offers an apparently insignificant yet telling description of the metaphorical status of the farm as wilderness: "an interval of two miles or so that separated us from the business district of the town, a distance never calculated exactly, because it wasn't a matter of space or time but one of difference" (9). She indirectly alludes to R. W. B. Lewis's justly renowned argument in *The American Adam* that canonical American heroes engage the quest in order to escape the limitation of time by crossing the border to the infinity of space. Time always catches up, of course, as Natty's death of old age at the conclusion of *The Prairie* shows, but the heroism lies in the effort. The passage just quoted, however, rejects the masculine dichotomy of space and time to stress the feminine insistence on difference. This is a gender issue that Gram personifies. Although she may act like a man with her bluster, authority, and power, she is nevertheless a mother, a heroine, and a woman. Dan's dubbing her Queen of Persia is part rueful regret, part admiration. She is the queen of the wilderness, and she engenders life in both her daughters and her fields. When she has to move on at the end of the adventure to trace, in Ishmael's words, "the round again," she glances back over her shoulder not with sentimentality but with satisfaction.

Chase is not interested in such simplicities of gender as nurturing women and negative men. Gram's daughters return home to die near her because the farm beyond the border has given them life, but the Queen is no literary grandmama, all bosom and grin and hugs. With food on the table and doctors on call she greets the sick and then sallies forth into the night for bingo, movies, or gambling. Nor does Chase characterize Gram as an advocate for such political chimeras as female solidarity. Despite her houseful of women and dismissal of men, she sees individuals rather than genders. When, for example, Celia—one of the collective "we"—matures into adolescence and breaks the bond with sisters and cousins by choosing to be with males, Gram does not circle the wagons against the masculine threat. The narrator, not the Queen, is upset at the relinquishing of relationship: "After that we tried to avoid Celia—who didn't care and always did exactly as she wished, all her energy and her allegiance straining away toward a destiny we did not share or even understand" (15).

Celia exacerbates the tensions not between men and women but between mothers and daughters. Her mother, Aunt Libby, accepts as natural all the bodily functions that define females, covering neither breasts nor articles of hygiene, explaining to the "we" that "being female was a dirty business, no use trying to hide it" (18). The girls see Libby as personifying the wisdom of an Edenic territory, as reflecting "the flickering shadows of woods," and thus they are astonished when she shouts "goddam" and "turd" at her husband Dan (18). But they also intuit that Libby is desirable and tempting, a woman who surprises them by denying the lure of romance which Celia readily accepts. Celia's awakening to sexuality urges Libby to expose the fallacies of the traditional female text that preaches the sanctity of marriage or the punishment of death. Faced with the daughter's romances and the "we's" naive belief that every woman has one true love who will find her, the mother longs not to reproduce mothering but to revise fiction instead:

> Wise and embittered herself, she [Libby] would deny us even our early innocence so that, just as she intended, we would never learn for ourselves the full fascination and implication of her knowledge. . . . She spoke to us incessantly of love. Endless betrayal. . . . Nor would Aunt

Libby allow us the miscalculation that marriage put an end to trouble.
(22, 24)

Chase's point is that female revision has its own extremes, its own ability to undermine women's bonding, which indeed occurs when the daughter frees the sexuality that the mother represses. In dramatizing this tension within female relationships Chase acknowledges a central tenet of feminist anthropologists that women choose mates rather than wait to be chosen: Celia unbuttons her blouse, undresses herself, draws the male toward her, and guides his mouth. Spying on their once bonded companion, their hearts plunging and thudding, the "we" rejects the mother's warnings to accept the daughter's individuality (34).

So does Gram. Proud of her eighty years, despite the traditional lesson that women should equate the advance of age with the loss of beauty, the Queen counsels on both the disappointments of marriage ("Lasts too long as it is") and the privileges of youth ("Have fun while you're young") (47). She understands that female bonding is imperfect because women react individually when personal desires are at stake. Thus, she is not at all surprised when the collective narrator describes itself as "Like selfish and evil stepsisters, spurned and embittered" after Celia's boyfriend prefers her instead of them (53). Always the pioneer, never afraid to face west, Gram takes Celia to Hawaii following the shock of a broken love affair. Her irony is that the adventure represents a honeymoon for Celia because a husband is *not* involved, but Chase's larger query is whether women fear beauty in another woman as threats to themselves. The imperfections of female relationships are such that the "we" welcomes Celia back to the fold only after she loses her looks.

A primary dilemma in *During the Reign of the Queen of Persia* is not how to avoid men but, rather, how to deal with them. Segregation of the sexes is a fantasy, as even Gram concedes when she blames males for turmoil in the territory yet understands that women and men will always desire each other. Sexual desire and bonding are not identical, and thus Gram can sympathize with Celia and simultaneously explain how she "puts" men where she wants them: "The way Gram told it was that all she had ever had in life was kids and work and useless men" (90). In her view of the male plot men either journey west and die or remain home and wither. Shaped by an absent father—by now a cliché in women's novels of the 1980s—and by a violent husband, Gram raises five daughters after two sons die in infancy. The lessons she carries with her to the wilderness of the farm are that men wander while women survive and that men are willful while women adapt.

For all its lovely prose, evocation of a moment forever lost in American culture, and sensitive account of the ebb and flow of generations, *During the Reign of the Queen of Persia* conveys an unexpected anger about both unstable female bonding and gender antipathy. The collective narrator recalls the endless tensions as merely a tale to be perused, as if reading sentimental fiction were still the way for women to become heroines: "To us it was all romantic and fun to think about, seemed scarcely to concern us, like fairy tales or cautionary fables that are not to be taken literally or to heart" (132). Reading life on the isolated farm as if it were the pages of an imaginary book, the girls cast Gram as the main character empowered to vanquish such male foils as Uncle Neil, who believes that men pick women for marriage and that "the female of the species in her native habitat" is both invigorating and grotesque (157).

Nowhere is gender exclusivity better illustrated than in the presence of death. The terminal illness of one of the narrator's aunts draws Gram's five daughters together with a solidarity that the "we" recognizes as loyalty only to each other and the mother. Faced with suffering and male intrusion, the mother-daughter bond closes ranks. Even the girls are turned away. Chase uses such words as *united* and *oneness* to suggest the integrity of the bond in the proximity of death. The children look at the dying aunt with awe: "And it was as though her presence and our devotion to her had united us at last in a perfect oneness, we four girls thinking, feeling and moving in a dimension that felt like the exact representation of a greater mind" (196). This mind is feminine, of course, all embracing, always nurturing when extreme crisis overwhelms tendencies to split the bond. Chase develops the exclusivity with a stark contrast: Gram's husband, Grandad, dies alone. No one "expects" him to die; no male comforts him; no female much notices. Gram's first thought is for his cows. The individual bond of masculinity which guards Natty-Chingachgook or Huck-Jim through the adventure is never a feature in *During the Reign of the Queen of Persia*. Chase's women rewrite the traditional male plot of the quest, place themselves in rooms with a "view of the west and the outlying woods beyond the meadows," and rein in maleness by framing a picture of an American Indian and hanging it over the mantel like a trophy (198). Women see golden bars of sunlight against the western forest line. Men face darkness and die alone.

But all is not pink ribbons and lace at the conclusion. Always aware of their lives as text, the "we" realizes that the end of the story means a rent in the bond. Relationship solidified in the presence of death weakens with the pressures of life. Gram is still the heroine in Chase's revision of the paradigm, but the quest means motion, and motion means change. Chase suggests that Gram's selling the land is both a gesture toward the future and a straining of the bond: "We were as separated from her as always, living on there, awaiting her decisions, with everything that happened heightened with the poignancy and solemnity of an old tale" (266). Chase writes the matriarch as the author of women's lives. Daughters tell the story, but mothers shape the text.

The irony is that the new heroine survives in an old woman. Lesser women lose both bond and vitality when they leave the wilderness represented by the farm. The final words of the novel are "closed the door," an indication that other quests require different tales. *During the Reign of the Queen of Persia* is, like *Housekeeping*, one of those rare novels that point to new possibilities in American literature, possibilities that include revising the fictionalization of gender and fiction itself.

Lisa Alther: *Other Women*

The marginalization of women traditionally results in the trivializing of women's fiction, but no more so than when a female author moves homosexual issues from the periphery to the center. Aware of the dilemma, Lisa Alther selects the title *Other Women* (1984) to stress the culturally determined double bind of females as Other and of lesbians as other females.[19] She investigates how the complexities of women's bonding involve both the sexual and the psychological when she creates Caroline Kelley as a heroine who turns to therapist Hannah Burke for help in picking up the pieces after the bond with her lover, Diana, is shattered. Female relationships alone, in other words, determine the boundaries of the new heroine's life. Gender exclusivity shapes gender politics to such an extreme that one wonders whether the resolution of Caroline's problem is too pat.

Several commentators think it is. Carol Sternhell, for instance, couches her analysis of *Other Women* as an ironic sigh of relief when she titles her essay "At Last, a Cure for Politics."[20] Observing of the 1980s that, "if the decade's gift to political discourse has been Reaganism, its contribution to literature may well be the therapy novel," she uses such words as *therapeutic platitudes* and *sappy* to criticize a novel that, she believes, undermines complex cultural issues (71). Christopher Lehmann-Haupt agrees.[21] Arguing that Alther overstates her case, Lehmann-Haupt complains that the reader feels manipulated by a tale that becomes increasingly didactic: "the dice are loaded. One of the more dramatic issues in the book is wheher Caroline is going to end up homosexual or not. But the three men in her life are all unpleasant caricatures . . . while the women are both various and appealing " (C16).

Polemic vies with art as a motivating factor in the novel. Yet it seems to me more useful, not to mention more accurate, to point out that the clash between politics and aesthetics in the technique of *Other Women* illustrates tensions in the thematics of the new heroine's life. The daughter of politically active parents, Caroline develops a fragile sense of self when she realizes that the parents' embrace of general causes masks their failure at personal love. Thus, Caroline would like to give her intimate relationships the perfection of art even while she feels guilty for spurning the imperfection of politics. Yet the complicating factor in her life, and in *Other Women*, is lesbianism, which is itself a political issue, a meeting ground of politics and intimacy. The complication is not new.

Blanche Wiesen Cook observes that, if all things were equal in literary history, 1928 would be celebrated as a banner year for lesbian writers.[22] Her evidence is the appearance of three unusual books: Virginia Woolf's *Orlando*, Djuna Barnes's *Ladies Almanack*, and Radclyffe Hall's *The Well of Loneliness*. But all things are not equal, and, thus, except for a limited readership, these fictions were suppressed, trivialized, or forgotten. The result, says Cook, is that lesbians grew up learning little about their sexual preference from literature. Even the books, much less the women, were Other: "for fifty years the variety of lesbian literature coexisted with the vigorous denial of lesbianism in general and the unending differences in manner and style among lesbian women in particular" (719). Cook equates the suppression of lesbian writing with the "historical denial" of women's history, and she argues that the censorship stems from a deliberate attempt to eliminate communities of women who reject self-definition according to proximity to men. Since the 1970s, however, the process of acknowledging the variations of lesbian literature has accelerated.[23]

Cook presumably sides with French—as opposed to American—feminist theorists when she insists not only that feminists begin with different interests and thus see with different sensibilities but also that "we seek, in fact, a different vocabulary" (728). One is uncertain whether she aligns feminism and lesbianism, but her statement illustrates the conflict discussed by Margaret Homans in the essay " 'Her Very Own Howl': The Ambiguities of Representation in Recent Women's Fiction" (which is discussed in chap. 4).[24] One of Cook's primary insights is that "heterosexist society" feels unthreatened by a lesbian relationship that appears to be culturally determined (730). She has in mind the acceptance and popularity of Gertrude Stein and Alice B. Toklas, but her observation is also relevant to novels about lesbians which were published in the 1980s and which have entered the literary mainstream.

Alther's *Other Women* is a case in point. A tale of female bonding, *Other Women* charts the heroine's vacillation between homosexuality and heterosexuality. Yet, significantly, the novel does not offend or even threaten most readers because the struggle of the lesbians is in part culturally determined. The principal "other" women, for example, have been married, raise children, work in the life-sustaining profession of nursing, and worry, as do millions of Americans, about the demands of being a single parent, and, thus, the primary means of financial support for the offspring. A heterosexual reader's sense of difference, of judging the lesbians in *Other Women* as dangerously deviant, is mitigated by the socially determined recognition of day-to-day problems shared by the population at large. Cook's indirect definition of lesbianism is relevant to Alther's novel: women "acting on behalf of their own needs, their own visions, and their own work" and not succumbing to historically prescribed roles that Cook unhesitatingly equates with patriarchy (735). The issue is not heterosexuality versus homosexuality but, rather, power. Independent access to and expression of eroticism *is* power. One need hardly stress that American culture has traditionally denied women such opportunity.

Other Women faces this issue with a therapist at the center. Janice Raymond coins the term *therapism*, by which she means "therapy as a way of life":[25]

> Therapism is an overvaluation of feeling. In a real sense, it is a tyranny of feelings where women have come to believe that what really counts in their life is their "psychology." And since they don't know what their psychology means, they submit to another who purports to know—a psychiatrist, counselor, or analyst. In this sense, we might say that therapism promotes a psychological hypochondria with women as the major seekers of emotional health. (155–56)

This is a significant point in *Other Women*, for, although she is a skilled nurse, Caroline Kelley resists terminating her therapy sessions. The reason is that she needs female friends at a time when her bonded companion has severed the tie. Thus, she seeks a female analyst, pays for the friendship by the hour, and manipulates her therapy, which is initiated by a broken bond in the first place, into a new relationship with a different female. Raymond argues that women substitute exploration of feelings for "passionate intimacy" when they enter therapy, and the result is "a loss of depth and a loss of intensity of female friendship" (159). Kelley's pursuit of erotic revelation with both men and women confirms her lack of confidence in the self. Her life is always relational. That is, she judges her value by her sexual appeal to others. Being both disciplined nurse and successful parent is not enough.

Hannah Burke understands the dilemma, but communicating her knowledge to Caroline is another matter: "Anyone who thought sex united people was out to lunch" (247). The problem, of course, at least as Alther presents it, is that lesbians *do* believe that sex can rally the marginalized to positions of power: "Jenny and Pam were close friends and occasional lovers. They devoted themselves to working for wages as little as possible, and to conducting as many simultaneous love affairs as they could. By not working they felt they did their bit toward undermining the patriarchy; by sharing the sexual wealth, they did their bit toward building the matriarchy" (98–99). The narrator apparently takes seriously such politically motivated bonding, but the reader wants to laugh as fiction gives way to polemic. On the one hand, Alther convincingly demonstrates how bonding turns into bondage when Caroline abandons detachment for entanglement, but, on the other hand, Alther veers toward editorializing when Caroline decides that homophobia is more serious than other social problems: "If you were black or crippled, at least your family still loved you. But if you were homosexual, you went it alone, as despised by your family as by the rest of society" (115–16).

Bonding, to Caroline, means not going it alone, but her relationships keep breaking down. She and her principal lover, Diana, react selfishly in areas of competition, especially sexual competition, and thus Alther develops the irony that lesbians marginalize each other when one accepts a man. Rather than homophobic, as is some traditional fiction, *Other Women* is often what one might call "malephobic." Although a nurse and thereby, ideally, a healer, Diana hates men. More to the point is that, like representative novels by women in the 1980s, *Other Women* begins by undermining the male. Before the end of the second page, for example, Caroline confronts the following variations of masculine violence: a child abused by an enraged father, her own situation as a mother of two children but without a husband, and a suicide by a male who drowns himself near her home in the woods of New Hampshire. To people from such urban centers as Boston, rural New England seems "like a barren wilderness inhabited by savages" (89). But to Caroline her house in the territory is like a revised Garden of Eden, which she recreates on a tapestry that features "both people women, both smiling and eating apples" (30). Paradise is the garden without the male.

One expects gender exclusivity in fiction that investigates female bonding from a lesbian perspective, but Alther suggests that women without men is an empowering model for females as various as the militantly antimale Diana, the bisexual Caroline, and the now happily married Hannah. Hannah, for instance, is abandoned by her father at five and widowed at nineteen. Presumably, such masculine desertion qualifies her to counsel women like Caroline who feel guilty for trying to revise gender roles prescribed by a society oriented toward male definitions of behavior. When Alther lists the multiple remedies culture offers unhappy women, she both smiles at Caroline and criticizes society: "marriage and motherhood, apple pie and monogamy, bigamy and polygamy; consumerism, communism, feminism, and God; sex, work, alcohol, drugs, and true love" (17). But, unlike Janice Raymond, Alther does not doubt the efficacy of psychotherapy for women who question their lives with men.

Caroline engages a psychiatrist because her bond with another woman fails. The tenuousness of female relationships is a dominant theme in contemporary American novels by women, and Alther stresses early in *Other Women* the connection between Diana's rebuffing Caroline and Caroline's recalling a baby girl deliberately burned by her father. Male abuse becomes a metaphor of female betrayal. It is as if women expect physical violence from men but are astonished at psychological mistreatment by women. The celebration of unshakable bonds in traditional American tales about men is not an issue in recent American novels about women.

Yet Alther does more than echo a persistent theme. She advances the intriguing notion that female nurturing is merely the other side of female selfishness. When anthropologists suggest that women bond imperfectly, they indicate the primacy of individual desire. Given such circumstances, one might define the instinct to nurture as a means of mitigating selfishness. But in Alther's portrayal of bonding nurturing enhances selfishness. Caroline and Diana split apart because each tries to outlove the other. Their mutual longings to love become so competitive that giving degenerates into taking:

> Their relationship wasn't working, they finally concluded, because each had an equivalent need to be needed. In relationships with men, each had been exploited to her heart's content. But with each other life was a constant struggle to outnurture. . . . Eventually they were compelled to address the issue of what to do about two people in whom thoughtfulness had become a disease. (29)

One cannot imagine similar motives breaking the bonds of Ike McCaslin and Sam Fathers or of Huck and Jim.

A nurturer by profession, Caroline sees her life's role as helping people feel better. To discover that giving can be selfish despite the culturally approved definition of women as helpmates is to confuse her sense of self. The psychotherapist's goal—and, by extension, Alther's point—is to persuade society that women are allowed to take instead of give. Note Caroline's reaction to Hannah's question "You don't see yourself as a taker?": "I'm a nurse, for God's sake. A mother" (45). But at the same time she is no virginal Natty Bumppo or innocent Huck Finn. Joining her peers, Alther revises the canon by rewriting the classics when she alludes to Hester Prynne as the archetypal character in Caroline's heritage. Like Hester, Caroline sews and weaves and thus recalls her stained progenitor as a marginalized woman who combines healing and art. Weaving to stave off despair, Caroline is a creator in her house at the edge of the clearing between the forest and the town, but, unlike Hester, she is not confident of who she is.

Caroline's turn toward men following the shattered relationship with women is Alther's means of indicating the unconfident female's need of approval by the dominant society. Psychotherapy helps Caroline shape her own sense of self, for Alther suggests that the only alternative is to let patriarchy form it for her. In other words, acceptance of men is an act of desperation despite the instability of female relationships. That she chooses a medical doctor for a liaison is Alther's irony: a female nurturer in need of nurturing selects a male who is supposed to nurture but who, instead, exploits. The doctor's first marriage has ended in divorce. His explanation is that he had to work overtime to pay for his wife's purchases; the wife's opinion is that he was never home. Recognizing in the doctor the syndrome of the absent male, Caroline nevertheless indulges him sexually because she knows that male-female relationships routinely have society's approval.

Developing Caroline's inability to read men, Alther apparently endorses the biodeterminist hypothesis that biology determines all gender differences. To support such anthropologists as Lionel Tiger and Robin Fox (their primary study is *The Imperial Animal*)[26] would seem counterproductive in a novel in praise of women, but Caroline accepts the biological roots of male aggression: "She'd spent her whole life rearing little boys, first her brothers and now her sons, and she still didn't understand them. Didn't understand their fascination with constructing elaborate machines for destruction from their Legos and Tinker Toys. . . . When she gave them dolls, as *Ms.* magazine recommended, they used them for target practice" (57). Having sex with a male is defining herself as a target. The unavoidable result is that a culturally sanctioned relationship increases her dependence on a socially disapproved bond. Longing for women, who betray her, she turns to men, who use her. Such is not always the case, of course, as

Hannah explains about Caroline's need of Diana, but the fact remains that, except for Hannah's second husband, all males in *Other Women* are repugnantly aggressive. Alther even goes so far as to echo Diane Johnson's *The Shadow Knows* when Caroline reads more than entertainment into the famous refrain from the radio program "The Shadow": "Who *knows* what evil lurks in the hearts of men?" (64).

The weakest parts of *Other Women* are Alther's descriptions of childhood trauma to account for adult fear: the absent father, the intimidating grandfather, the distant mother. More successful is her position that women traditionally read sentimental fiction to discover women's lives. Heroines need stories in order to be heroic, but they are unlikely to find suitable models in the American canon. Hannah recognizes this desire, and thus she peruses romances not to help herself but to read her patients. Acknowledging their longing for a new text and their inability to write it, she learns that sentimental fiction provides an unaggressive means of gender exclusivity: "She'd begun reading romances years ago, to find out what many of her female clients saw in them. She quickly understood they devoured them to convince themselves of the glamour of dreary marriages and boring or abusive husbands" (76). Sentimental novels highlight women, denigrate men, and manipulate heroines toward a happy ending. Much contemporary women's fiction eliminates the latter but revises the canon by appropriating similar dichotomies of gender.

Lesbianism complicates Caroline's reading of the text. That romantic novels privilege women over men is one thing, a celebration that Caroline can approve. But sexual preference isolates her from most women and thereby leaves her thinking that she can bond with no one. Both Caroline and *Other Women* are defensive:

> Caroline knew that a woman who hadn't felt desire for another woman regarded lesbianism as an inferior form of sexuality, fit only for the unfeminine and the immature. This was incorrect, but you couldn't tell hardened heterosexuals anything. They had biology . . . on their side. . . . There was no one in her life who thought lesbianism was fine except her lesbian friends. (85)

Her obsession with nurturing reflects the other side of her need to be nurtured, to form a relationship as inviolate as that of Natty and Chingachgook.

Thus, Alther directs the second half of *Other Women* to forming a bond between Caroline and Hannah, a kind of asexual tie made canonical by nineteenth-century male novelists. The foundation of the bond is not merely the dependence of patient on therapist but also Hannah's concession that gender differences are biologically based. Happily married, she joins Caroline in arguing that evolution favors males:

> It simply wasn't fair. Arthur [Hannah's husband] came by his steadiness biologically. Women, with their hormone storms, were in constant flux. In therapy she often prodded the men to allow themselves a wider emotional range, whereas the women usually needed to discover the part of themselves that didn't change along with the hormones each month. Until they found this inner pole star, they clung to relationships, or to anything else that seemed to promise external stability. (93)

In other words, the impetus for female bonding is the unfairness of biology. "External stability" may be a chimera, but canonical American novelists have made it a reality in fiction by aligning it with male bonding. Women have a more difficult time, as Tiger and Fox, and Sarah Hrdy, have observed.

Although Alther may be inadvertently ironic, she shows that the basis of the bond between Caroline and Hannah is not comaraderie and trust but, rather, suffering and loss. Hannah has endured the death of her first husband in a war and the deaths of two children in an accident, and thus she has experienced traumas similar to those that urge female patients to seek relationships with her. Such bonding is temporary, as Alther surely understands, but in *Other Women* it is all women have, given the general unreliability of female ties. As a therapist, Hannah becomes an ultimate mother in order to compensate for the loss of her two children, while Caroline quests for companions like Hannah in order to nullify the emotional distance from her own mother. In one sense, Alther offers a variation on Chodorow's thesis of the reproduction of mothering, but the more significant point is that the therapist nurtures a bond with the patient so that the latter becomes strong enough to break it.

Alther develops Caroline toward that moment by emphasizing malephobia to such an extent that the novel approaches propaganda. Women turn against Caroline for turning to men, even to the extreme of denying sympathy. In doing so they act out Hrdy's observation about the conflict between selfishness and bonding:

> "No thanks, Jenny, I just want some sympathy."
> "Well, you're not getting any from me, darling. Anyone who goes out with a man when she should know better deserves whatever she gets." (146)

At one moment in her despair over women's relationships Caroline even decides that not capitalism, racism, or nationalism but men are the primary cause of all conflict. Pregnancy is solely the man's fault; nuclear missiles are launched by men, who are otherwise impotent; fathers turn sons into rampaging man-the-hunter by giving them BB guns. Mitigating such political simplicity is Alther's wry assessment of the roles society reserves for women. Culture traditionally writes a text that assigns heroics to men. Women may become heroines only by proximity to a main character, who is always male. Caroline looks to the text to redefine herself but finds nothing: "If she wasn't Maid Marian to . . . Robin Hood, who was she? A boring little bourgeois housewife" (222). Caught between despicable men and second-rate heroines, she becomes Alther's version of woman-the-hunter when she picks up a female for a one-night stand: "There was only the present moment, and two healthy female animals, who had begun to explore each other with mouths and hands, like lost prospectors finding a water hole in the desert" (226).

Sexual prowling does not facilitate relationship, however, and Alther argues in the final movement of the novel that bonding with others requires sureness of self. The therapist forges the tie, shores up the individual, then nudges the patient to cut the knot. Janice Raymond would term Caroline's dependence on Hannah "psychological hypochondria," but Alther suggests that intense female friendships first necessitate definition of self, which a therapist can encourage. Self-love is not a flaw but a need, an initial step away from women's obsession with nurturing. Taking, indeed, may be a prerequisite for giving. When the bond with Diana dissolves for the last time, Alther indicates both the instability of women's relationships and the capability of women to stand alone. In canonical American fiction Natty always has Chingachgook *(The Last of the Mohicans)*, Huck always has Jim *(Adventures of Huckleberry Finn)*, Ike always has Sam *(Go Down, Moses)*, Sal always has Dean *(On the Road)*, and Ed Gentry always has Lewis Medlock *(Deliverance)*, at least until death intervenes. Contemporary American novels by men add women to the bond. Owen Meany always has John Wheelwright and Hester *(A Prayer for Owen Meany)* Petey always has Pop and Lizzie Bean *(Sometimes I Live in the Country)*, Ned always has Sam and Jenny *(The Risk Pool)*, Jerome always has Charles and Alpha *(Born Brothers)*, and Simons always has Taurus and the Duchess *(Edisto)*. Such stability is uncommon in women's novels of the 1980s. Lisa Alther and her peers have revised the text.

Notes

1. Mona Simpson, *Anywhere but Here* (1986; New York: Vintage, 1988). Although Simpson includes other first-person narrators, the story belongs to Ann.

2. "Mona (Elizabeth) Simpson," *Contemporary Literary Criticism Yearbook 1986*, ed. Sharon K. Hall (Kansas City, Mo.: Gale, 1987), 97.

3. Le Anne Schreiber, "In Thrall to a Lethal Mother," *New York Times Book Review* (11 January 1987): 7; quoted in "Mona (Elizabeth) Simpson," 101.

4. Dana A. Heller, *The Feminization of Quest-Romance: Radical Departures* (Austin: University of Texas Press, 1990), 117.

5. Deborah Denenholz Morse, "The Difficult Journey Home: Mona Simpson's *Anywhere but Here*," in *Mother Puzzles: Daughters and Mothers in Contemporary American Literature*, ed. Mickey Pearlman (Westport, Conn.: Greenwood, 1989), 67–75.

6. Hilma Wolitzer, *Hearts* (1980; New York: Ivy/Ballantine, 1990).

7. Elizabeth Pochoda, "Love Deciphered," *Ms.* 9 (December 1980): 38.

8. See Sarah Blaffer Hrdy, *The Woman That Never Evolved* (Cambridge: Harvard University Press, 1981).

9. *"Hearts," Virginia Quarterly Review* 57 (Summer 1981): 102.

10. Meg Wolitzer, *This Is Your Life* (1988; New York: Penguin, 1989).

11. Michiko Kakutani, "A Comedy of Contemporary Manners and Effluvia," *New York Times* (late ed.), 5 October 1988: C25; Jane De Lynn, "Can a Fat Girl Find Love?" *Los Angeles Times Book Review* (9 October 1988): 8; Susan Brownmiller, "A Comedian's Kids Learn Life Is No Joke," *Chicago Tribune Books* (16 October 1988): 8.

12. See chapters 2 and 3 of my *Women Enter the Wilderness: Male Bonding and the American Novel of the 1980s* (Columbia: University of South Carolina Press, 1991).

13. Lionel Tiger, *Men in Groups* (New York: Random House, 1969).

14. Joan Chase, *During the Reign of the Queen of Persia* (1983; New York: Ballantine, 1989).

15. Margaret Atwood, "Romantic Idealism, Barnyard Realism," *New York Times Book Review* (12 June 1983): 9.

16. Ellen Sweet, "During the Reign of the Queen of Persia," *Ms.* 13 (July 1984): 30.

17. Fran R. Schumer, "Midwestern Matriarch," *Nation* (10 September 1983): 187.

18. See also Schumer: "Not since *The New Yorker* expropriated the 'we' pronoun for its Talk of the Town has anyone managed to use it as gracefully as Joan Chase in this evocative first novel" (187).

19. Lisa Alther, *Other Women* (1984; New York: Signet, 1985).

20. Carol Sternhell, "At Last, a Cure for Politics," *Village Voice* (18 December 1984): 71.

21. Christopher Lehmann-Haupt, "Books of the Times," *New York Times*, 10 December 1984: C16.

22. Blanche Wiesen Cook, "'Women Alone Stir My Imagination': Lesbianism and the Cultural Tradition," *Signs* 4 (Summer 1979): 718–39.

23. Cook praises especially the Arno Press reprint series, *Homosexuality: Lesbians and Gay Men in Society, History and Literature.*

24. Margaret Homans, "'Her Very Own Howl': The Ambiguities of Representation in Recent Women's Fiction," *Signs* 9 (Winter 1983): 185–205.

25. Janice G. Raymond, *A Passion for Friends: Toward a Philosophy of Female Affection* (Boston: Beacon Press, 1986), 155.

26. Lionel Tiger and Robin Fox, *The Imperial Animal* (New York: Holt, Rinehart and Winston, 1971).

Chapter Seven

Coda: Douglas Ungar, Male Novelists, Wilderness Women

Women in the wilderness is not a common topic in contemporary American novels by men except when the novels feature male bonding. In canonical American fiction James Fenimore Cooper, Herman Melville, and Mark Twain send their bonded companions across the border into the territory of everlasting possibility to quest for an elusive freedom, which translates into an avoidance of women. If females dare to enter the wilderness, as does Cooper's Cora, they are either killed in the dark forest or returned to the tame settlement. Heroic behavior is not for women when the quest is a male prerogative. Male novelists of the 1980s revise this venerable paradigm by showing that women are necessary to the stability of masculine relationships on the far side of society. Richard Russo, John Irving, and Frederick Busch celebrate the presence of women in the territory, even while they extend the paradigmatic theme of men leaving home for the long journey. That contemporary female novelists have revised the canon by rewriting rather than repudiating the text is a major point of my study. But what happens when a recent male author features women in the wilderness without the traditional frame of male bonding? Douglas Ungar probes this question in *Leaving the Land* (1984).[1]

A native of Moscow, Idaho, Ungar has lived the adventure that canonical novelists immortalize and contemporary novelists imagine. Formerly the manager of a sheep ranch and the owner of a homestead in the far west, he has worked the mythical territory that continues to shape the American imagination. The germ of *Leaving the Land* was Ungar's struggle to pay the taxes levied on his farm by both state and federal agencies, but in converting fact to fiction he created a heroine—Marge Hogan—who feels stuck between the patriarchal requirement that she marry and the feminist mandate that she be free to roam.

Leaving the Land owes as much to novels by women as to myths by men. Set in South Dakota after the Great Depression, Ungar's tale uses a lyrical tone to investigate a social tragedy: the decline of family homesteads due to the rise of impersonal business. At one end of the literary spectrum stands Willa Cather's *O Pioneers!* (1913), with the ironic contrast that Cather lauds the beginning of the adventure while Ungar laments the conclusion. At the other end is Joan Chase's *During the Reign of the Queen of Persia,* which, like *Leaving the Land,* features an elegiac quality created by the interplay between nature's rhythms and humanity's loss. Ungar's heroine works the farm as hard as Cather's women, and she honors family as fervently as Chase's matriarchy. Yet her urge to leave the territory metaphorically precipitates the demise of the very land that gives her a room of her own: she marries Jim Vogel, the attorney for an agribusiness that obliterates family farms. This is not to suggest that Ungar romanticizes Marge Hogan or visualizes a latter-day Scarlett O'Hara vowing never to be hungry again. Willing to work but longing to love, Marge is also, as John McInerney observes, "mud-spattered, bloodied, dung-stained, humiliated, and demeaned."[2] Worse, she is alone, denied the bond, however tenuous, with other women which female novelists of the 1980s feature to varying degrees.

How, then, does a contemporary male writer treat the gender issue of wilderness women? First, he eliminates female relationships to emphasize the isolation of life in the wild, then he reverses the quest to show the heroine leaving the adventure tale in the territory for the domestic plot in the town. True to heroines in traditional novels, Marge is taught to believe that the life of an unmarried female is a sign of failure: "She was terrified. She grew convinced, for the first time, that she was doomed to live as a solitary woman for the rest of her life" (40). Ungar comically undercuts a culture that writes the closure of marriage as the conclusion of the text. Marge puts on new clothes, drives from the farm to the town, sits on a bar stool, crosses her legs, arranges her hair over one eye, flares her nostrils, exudes clouds of cigarette smoke, unhooks the top buttons of her dress, and flutters her eyes—just as a heroine is supposed to do in a romance novel. But, while charting Marge's pursuit of men, Ungar simultaneously revises her role as a nineteenth-century sentimental heroine. When, for example, a man addresses her with the masculine clichés of endearment, she responds as a person more at home on the land than in the parlor: "I'm not any goddamned *gal*" (42).

The point from the perspective of the male novelist is that the contemporary woman who crosses the border finds herself between texts. Raised, on the one hand, according to the prescriptions of the sentimental novel, she is supposed to reproduce mothering by staying in the home. Intuiting, on the other hand, the revision of the marriage plot, she longs to establish independence by engaging the quest. As Ungar develops the relationship between women and fiction, the traditional novel needs rewriting, but the new narrative has yet to be composed. Thus, he sets the beginning of *Leaving the Land* during World War II, indicating war as the ultimate male quest, and he then traces Marge's life following the deaths of her bonded brothers in battle. Like American female novelists of the 1980s, Ungar characterizes men as either absent or foolish, but, unlike his female peers, he does not offer women without men as the natural means of revising the canon.

Feisty, independent Marge spars with a father who insists that she marry. The kind of man who built the country by wrenching a homestead from the wild west, Ben Hogan believes in the veracity of the canonical tale: women who come home early "won't get nobody" (6). He means a man, of course, which, according to a male quester such as himself, all women should want. But Ungar's irony is that, in allowing the daughter to work beside the sons, the father inadvertently shows her the adventures beyond the home. Ungar uses accounts of Marge's chores to illustrate his sense of the new heroine caught between two texts: she knows how to hunt with her brothers and to handle wrenches for their machines, but she is also expected to cook their breakfast. In Ungar's portrayal of gender relationships mothers shape daughters to emulate themselves. Since Marge's mother is a kitchen woman, a female trained to work for rather than with males, Marge has difficulty revising her life without rebuffing her parent. The word *imprisoned* in the following account of the daughter's dilemma pinpoints the tension between the genders: "She didn't mind cooking, cleaning and canning, would never have thought to mind it, but she felt imprisoned by the kitchen as her men worked. She would much rather have been out there with them. . . . She chewed their tobacco" (22). The outbreak of World War II releases her to what she thinks is freedom in the fields, for the sons hurry to the "great adventure" of battle, but once there she longs to escape to the town.

From the male novelist's perspective the new female is alone because she lacks models. Marge's father believes that a woman who tills the land is unladylike. Marge's mother believes that a woman who resists marriage will have no man to take care of her. Marge herself believes that a woman who rallies to other females just because available men have gone to war is a hypocrite: "She couldn't help but begin to hate that crowd of women" (32). Surviving in the wilderness by working the farm like a man, she nevertheless dreams of romance by rewriting herself as a heroine. Yet the men to whom she offers herself are selfish, unfeeling, and coarse. Reversing the structure of the canonical novel, which frees men to the territory and relegates women to the community, Ungar suggests that the town represents the quest for a woman of the wilderness who is bonded to no one. The other side of the border means nothing but hard work.

Thus, when a dark stranger roars into town with a black convertible and sunglasses—clearly Ungar's parody of old westerns—Marge becomes a kind of Miss Kitty to his Marshall Dillon, except that she marries him. More to the point is that Marge responds to Jim Vogel as if he were the mysterious lover in a sentimental romance whose primary narrative function is to coerce the heroine to the closure of marriage. In terms of the plot of *Leaving the Land* Marge's affair with Vogel signals disaster, since he litigates judicial matters for the business conglomerate that purchases small farms. In terms of the relation between gender and fiction, however, the marriage is more significant. Unlike his female counterparts, Ungar *begins* with a woman in the wilderness, but he also shows that crossing the border does not necessarily mean rewriting the canon. Marge's desire for traditional romance is the exact opposite of the longings of Marilynne Robinson's heroines, and her marriage to Vogel illustrates the enormity of her misreading of the text. Her efforts to leave the land by love and marriage are thwarted by the obtuseness of males who want to strut their stuff like the foolish turkeys raised on the local farms. Convinced that hunting with her brothers initiates her to the role of adventuring heroine, she walks from the farm into the pages of the traditional novel. Ungar's unexpected irony suggests not only the power of the marriage plot but also the contemporary male novelist's sense that woman's quest is difficult to sustain. This is because the characteristics of the masculine narrative challenge the woman who would revise them. Even the local hospital is the domain of male adventure with its howitzer shell for an ashtray, its picture of an American Indian on a plunging horse, its portrait of fringed pioneers in a buffalo-hide dinghy, and its "genuine framed replica of Wild Bill Hickok's last poker hand" (84). These mementos of the paradigmatic American novel would be placed over a fireplace in such a tale as *During the Reign of the Queen of Persia*, but the male writer suggests that rethinking the canon is not so easy.

Ungar recognizes the double bind that men impose on women. The father urges the daughter to marry as fulfillment of the female role, but he becomes angry when she chooses a man. Tarnished as if she were a piece of silver, she can "never be his little girl again" (93). The irony from the male novelist's point of view is clear: the woman rebels against parental pressure by selecting her own mate, but the

rebellion does no more than limit her to the marriage tale of the conventional narrative. Whereas contemporary female novelists watch
heroines cross the bridge with Marilynne Robinson or take to the road
with Mona Simpson, Ungar stresses the difficulty of completing the
journey. Lighting out for the territory to engage the quest is not a
natural decision for a woman when a man writes the tale. Marge can
join the Waves, apply to beauty school, or just pack up and leave, but
without a bonded companion she would be entirely on her own. Even
in the "postfeminist" era male writers hesitate to challenge the canon
except when they focus on relationships among men which women
solidify—as in *A Prayer for Owen Meany* or *Sometimes I Live in the Country.*

Where Ungar and his female peers agree is about the limitation
of marriage. Rather than an escape from the land, Marge's wedding
formalizes an incarceration in the kitchen. She dusts the furniture,
folds the laundry, and cooks the meals, just as conventional fiction has
taught her. Her honeymoon hotel reiterates the primacy of the canonical novel, crammed as it is with hunting scenes on the wall and conven-
tioneers in the corridors. Ungar exposes the gender expectations of
marriage as radically as female novelists. Once married, for example,
Vogel reestablishes the male bond. He "almost never came home early.
He was the kind of man who settled deeply into conversation whether
it concerned his business or just the tales and outright lies of farmers,
ranchers, and range boys at the bar. He seemed able to laugh easily
in bars when he seldom laughed anywhere else" (130). He assumes
that commerce and politics are the natural arenas of male expertise,
and he is baffled when his wife watches *The Best Years of Our Lives,* a
classic movie of male bonding, in an effort to determine the cause of
her discomfort. The culprit, of course, is marriage itself, and thus
Ungar develops the second half of *Leaving the Land* around Marge's
effort to hold onto the land she once had but has spurned. Divorce
from Vogel parallels disintegration of the farms, and Ungar stresses the
isolation of the female who remains in the territory without husband
or bonded companions. Female novelists of the 1980s emphasize either
the effort of women to enter a territory long thought to be the space
of male privilege *(Housekeeping, Hearts)* or the difficulty of maintaining
relationships once women take to the road *(Anywhere but Here, Other
Women).* In both instances males are repudiated and female bonds
broken.

A representative male novelist with similar concerns, Ungar suggests the confusion a heroine must confront when she tries to rewrite
the old text without adequately preparing the new. He uses Marge's
ostentatious house in town to illustrate the dilemma. Having aban-

doned the farm to chart what she believes is her own journey, Marge becomes trapped in the patriarchal narrative. As she tells her son, "This is the house where I woke up one morning spiritually dead" (157). At the center of the house is Vogel's study complete with army medals, antique swords, and rifles. Women and children are not welcome in the room, the lair of man-the-hunter, a situation that recalls Cooper's banishing Cora and Alice from the wilderness or Melville's refusing to let women enter at all. From the male writer's point of view—but not the female's—a heroine in the territory longs for a man in the town. The desire for romance—the reversed quest, as it were—remains the lure for even the most independent woman. Leaving the land means leaving the future: "There is an immortality given to the earth, a sense of expansive dream passed from immigrant homesteader through generation after generation of his children in a self-perpetuating vision of the meaning of freedom and wealth" (208). Given the opportunity to be Cora Munro, Marge unfortunately chooses to become Alice. Her heroism is her effort to return to the land, to pass it on to her son.

Only at the end of the novel, and near the end of her life, does she concede the inadequacy of the marriage plot. Free of her husband but also, significantly, shorn of female relationships, Marge accepts her predicament as a woman stranded between two tales, the outmoded narrative and the one yet to be written: "I've learned to like to be alone. And I could have done it out here alone, once. But I never would have thought of it then. I always thought I needed a man and just couldn't find the right one" (311). American female novelists of the 1980s would agree that the new heroine does not need a man, but, unlike Ungar, they would suggest that the narrative necessary to accommodate such a woman has already been composed.

That a different narrative has been written is a primary contribution to American fiction. Reinventing the heroine by rewriting the quest, female novelists of the 1980s have revised a paradigm that has directed American literature for more than two centuries. Rather than reject a literary tradition responsible in part for shaping the national culture, contemporary female writers adapt the male plot of freeing bonded companions from social restraint by sending them into the wilderness. Whereas such canonical novelists as Cooper, Twain, and Faulkner leave the woman behind, such recent authors as Irving, Woiwode, and Busch want the woman with them. The latter group repudiates the gender gap that the former emphasizes. But female novelists have reopened the gap. Reading Joan Chase, Mona Simpson, Marilynne Robinson, and the other writers discussed here, one wonders whether the central issue in contemporary women's writing is the formalization of a new gender exclusivity just at the moment when separation of the sexes in novels is being challenged by men.

Notes

1. Douglas Ungar, *Leaving the Land* (1984; New York: Ballantine, 1988).

2. John McInerney, review of *Leaving the Land* by Douglas Unger, *Best Sellers*, 44 (April 1984): 10–11.

Sources

Abel, Elizabeth. "(E)Merging Identities: The Dynamics of Female Friendship in Contemporary Fiction by Women." *Signs* 6 (Spring 1981): 413–35.

Abraham, Laurie, Mary Beth Danielson, Nancy Eberle, Laura Green, Janice Rosenberg, and Carroll Stoner. *Reinventing Home: Six Working Women Look at Their Home Lives*. New York: Plume, 1991.

Aldrich, Marcia. "The Poetics of Transience: Marilynne Robinson's *Housekeeping*." *Essays in Literature* 16 (Spring 1989): 127–40.

Alther, Lisa. *Other Women*. 1984; New York: Signet, 1985.

Atwood, Margaret. "Romantic Idealism, Barnyard Realism." *New York Times Book Review* (12 June 1983): 9, 40.

Auerbach, Nina. *Communities of Women: An Idea of Fiction*. Cambridge, Mass.: Harvard University Press, 1978.

Baker, Paula. *The Moral Frameworks of Public Life: Gender, Politics, and the State of Rural New York, 1870–1930*. New York: Oxford University Press, 1991.

Bleier, Ruth. *Science and Gender: A Critique of Biology and Its Theories on Women*. New York: Pergamon, 1984.

Brownmiller, Susan. "A Comedian's Kids Learn Life Is No Joke." *Chicago Tribune Books* (16 October 1988): 8.

Brownstein, Rachel M. *Becoming a Heroine: Reading about Women in Novels*. New York: Viking, 1982.

Busch, Frederick. *Sometimes I Live in the Country*. Boston: Godine, 1986.

Caplan, Brina. "It Is Better to Have Nothing." *Nation* 232 (7 February 1981): 152, 154.

Chase, Joan. *During the Reign of the Queen of Persia*. 1983; New York: Ballantine, 1989.

Chodorow, Nancy. *The Reproduction of Mothering: Psychoanalysis and the Sociology of Gender*. 1978; Berkeley: University of California Press, 1979.

Chopin, Kate. *The Awakening*. Ed. Margaret Culley. 1899; New York: W. W. Norton, 1976.

Cook, Blanche Wiesen. "'Women Alone Stir My Imagination': Lesbianism and the Cultural Tradition." *Signs* 4 (Summer 1979): 718–39.

Davies, Russell. "On the Verge of Collapse." *Times Literary Supplement* (8 July 1977): 821.

De Lynn, Jane. "Can a Fat Girl Find Love?" *Los Angeles Times Book Review* (9 October 1988): 8.

Dickey, James. *Deliverance*. Boston: Houghton Mifflin, 1970.

Didion, Joan. *A Book of Common Prayer*. 1977; New York: Pocket Books, 1978.

Di Filippo, Dana, and Laura E. Wexler. "Feminist Movement May Suffer as Today's Students Shun Label." *U: The National College Newspaper*, March 1991, 1–2.

Dinnerstein, Dorothy. *The Mermaid and the Minotaur: Sexual Arrangements and Human Malaise*. New York: Harper and Row, 1976.

Dworkin, Andrea. *Mercy*. New York: Four Walls Eight Windows, 1991.

Edwards, Thomas R. "Academic Vaudeville." *New York Review of Books* (20 February 1975): 34–35.

Foster, Thomas. "History, Critical Theory, and Women's Social Practices: 'Women's Time' and *Housekeeping*." *Signs* 14 (Autumn 1988): 73–99.

Friedman, Ellen G., ed. *Joan Didion: Essays and Conversations*. Princeton, N.J.: Ontario Review Press, 1984.

Gardiner, Judith Kegan. "The (US)es of (I)dentity: A Response to Abel on '(E)Merging Identities.'" *Signs* 6 (Spring 1981): 436–44.

———. "On Female Identity and Writing by Women." *Critical Inquiry* 8 (Winter 1981): 347–61.

Gehr, Richard. "Sins of the Flesh Eaters: Marianne Wiggins's Carnal Knowledge." *Village Voice* (21 March 1989): 50.

Greiner, Donald J. *Women Enter the Wilderness: Male Bonding and the American Novel of the 1980s*. Columbia: University of South Carolina Press, 1991.

Hanley, Lynne T. "To El Salvador." *Massachusetts Review* 24 (Spring 1983): 13–29.

Haraway, Donna J. "In the Beginning Was the Word: The Genesis of Biological Theory." *Signs* 6 (Spring 1981): 469–81.

Harris, Susan K. "'But is it any *good*?': Evaluating Nineteenth-Century American Women's Fiction." *American Literature* 63 (March 1991): 43–61.

Haynes, Muriel. "What Evil Lurks. . . ." *Ms.* 3 (November 1974): 37–38, 40.

"Hearts." *Virginia Quarterly Review* 57 (Summer 1981): 102.

Heilbrun, Carolyn G. *Hamlet's Mother and Other Women*. 1990; New York: Ballantine, 1991.

———. *Reinventing Womanhood*. New York: W. W. Norton, 1979.

———. *Writing a Woman's Life*. 1988; New York: Ballantine, 1989.

Heise, Lori. "The Global War against Women." *Washington Post*, 9 April 1989, B1.

Heller, Dana. *The Feminization of Quest-Romance: Radical Departures*. Austin: University of Texas Press, 1990.

Hollowell, John. "Against Interpretation: Narrative Strategy in *A Book of Common Prayer*." In *Joan Didion: Essays and Conversations*, ed. Ellen G. Friedman, 164–76. Princeton, N.J.: Ontario Review Press, 1984.

Homans, Margaret. "'Her Very Own Howl': The Ambiguities of Representation in Recent Women's Fiction." *Signs* 9 (Winter 1983): 186–205.

Hrdy, Sarah Blaffer. *The Woman That Never Evolved*. Cambridge, Mass.: Harvard University Press, 1981.

Irving, John. *A Prayer for Owen Meany*. New York: Morrow, 1989.

Iyer, Pico. "Are Men Really So Bad?" *Time* (22 April 1991): 94.

Jacobus, Mary. *Reading Women*. New York: Columbia University Press, 1986.

Johnson, Diane. "Hard Hit Women." *New York Review of Books* (28 April 1977): 6, 8.

———. *The Shadows Knows*. 1974; New York: Vintage, 1982.

Kakutani, Michiko. "A Comedy of Contemporary Manners and Effluvia." *New York Times* (late ed.), 5 October 1988, C25.

Kavanagh, Julie. "Escaping into Flux." *Times Literary Supplement* (3 April 1981): 371.

Kerouac, Jack. *On the Road*. 1957; New York: Viking Compass, 1962.

Kimmel, Michael S. "Music of the Spheres." *Nation* 12, no. 19 (August 1991): 205–8.

Kirkby, Joan. "Is There Life after Art? The Metaphysics of Marilynne Robinson's *Housekeeping*." *Tulsa Studies in Women's Literature* 5 (Spring 1986): 91–109.

Kraf, Elaine. *Princess of Seventy-second Street*. New York: New Directions, 1979.

Lassner, Phyllis. "Escaping the Mirror of Sameness: Marilynne Robinson's *Housekeeping*." In *Mother Puzzles: Daughters and Mothers in Contemporary American Literature*, ed. Mickey Pearlman, 49–58. Westport, Conn.: Greenwood Press, 1989.

Lehmann-Haupt, Christopher. "Books of the Times." *New York Times*, 10 December 1984, C16.

Lewis, R. W. B. *The American Adam: Innocence, Tragedy, and Tradition in the Nineteenth Century*. 1955; Chicago: University of Chicago Press, 1964.

McInerney, John. Review of *Leaving the Land*, by Douglas Ungar. *Best Sellers* 44 (April 1984): 10–11.

"Marilynne Robinson." In *Conversations with Contemporary American Writers*, New Series 50, ed. Sanford Pinsker. Amsterdam: Costerus, 1985.

Meese, Elizabeth A. *Crossing the Double-Cross: The Practice of Feminist Criticism*. Chapel Hill: University of North Carolina Press, 1986.

Merchant, Carolyn. *The Death of Nature: Women, Ecology and the Scientific Revolution*. San Francisco: Harper and Row, 1980.

"Mona (Elizabeth) Simpson." *Contemporary Literary Criticism Yearbook 1986*, ed. Sharon K. Hall, 97–103. Kansas City, Mo.: Gale, 1987.

Morse, Deborah Denenholz. "The Difficult Journey Home: Mona Simpson's *Anywhere but Here*." In *Mother Puzzles: Daughters and Mothers in Contemporary American Literature*, ed. Mickey Pearlman, 67–75 Westport, Conn.: Greenwood Press, 1989.

Naylor, Gloria. *The Women of Brewster Place*. 1982; New York: Penguin, 1985.

Ownby, Ted. *Subduing Satan: Religion, Recreation and Manhood in the Rural South, 1865–1920*. Chapel Hill: University of North Carolina Press, 1991.

Pochoda, Elizabeth. "Love Deciphered." *Ms.* 9 (December 1980): 38–39.

Powell, Padgett. *Edisto*. New York: Farrar, Straus and Giroux. 1984.

Rafferty, Terrence. "Outlaw Princesses." *New Yorker* (3 June 1991): 86–87.

Ravits, Martha. "Extending the American Range: Marilynne Robinson's *Housekeeping*." *American Literature* 61 (December 1989): 644–66.

Raymond, Janice G. *A Passion for Friends: Toward a Philosophy of Female Affection*. Boston: Beacon Press, 1986.

Rich, Adrienne. *Of Woman Born: Motherhood as Experience and Institution*. New York: W. W. Norton, 1976.

Robinson, Marilynne. *Housekeeping*. 1981; New York: Bantam, 1984.

———. "So Where Does a Writer's Influence Come From?" *Ms.* (August 1984): 112.

Rossner, Judith. *Looking for Mr. Goodbar*. New York: Simon and Schuster, 1975.

Russo, Richard. *The Risk Pool*. New York: Random House, 1988.

Ryan, Maureen. "Marilynne Robinson's *Housekeeping:* The Subversive Narrative and the New American Eve." *South Atlantic Review* 56 (January 1991): 79–86.

Schickel, Richard. "Gender Bender." *Time* (24 June 1991): 52–56.

Schreiber, Le Anne. "In Thrall to a Lethal Mother." *New York Times Book Review* (11 January 1987): 7.

Schumer, Fran R. "Midwestern Matriarch." *Nation* (10 September 1983): 187.

Sedgwick, Eve Kosofsky. *Between Men: English Literature and Male Homosocial Desire*. New York: Columbia University Press, 1985.

Simpson, Mona. *Anywhere but Here*. 1986; New York: Vintage, 1988.

Stack, Carol B. *All Our Kin: Strategies for Survival in a Black Community*. New York: Harper and Row, 1974.

Steiner, Wendy. "Declaring War on Men." *New York Times Book Review* (15 September 1991): 11.

Sternhell, Carol. "At Last, a Cure for Politics." *Village Voice* (18 December 1984): 71.

Strandberg, Victor. "Passion and Delusion in *A Book of Common Prayer.*" In *Joan Didion: Essays and Conversations*, ed. Ellen G. Friedman, 147–63. Princeton, N.J.: Ontario Review Press, 1984.

Sweet, Ellen. "During the Reign of the Queen of Persia." *Ms.* 13 (July 1984): 30-31.

Tanner, Laura E. "Reading Rape: *Sanctuary* and *The Women of Brewster Place.*" *American Literature* 62 (December 1990): 559–82.

Tiger, Lionel. *Men in Groups.* New York: Random House, 1969.

Tiger, Lionel, and Robin Fox. *The Imperial Animal.* New York: Holt, Rinehart and Winston, 1971.

Ungar, Douglas. *Leaving the Land.* 1984; New York: Ballantine, 1988.

Wiggins, Marianne. *John Dollar.* New York: Harper and Row, 1989.

Woiwode, Larry. *Born Brothers.* New York: Farrar, Straus and Giroux, 1988.

Wolitzer, Hilma. *Hearts.* 1980; New York: Ivy/Ballantine, 1990.

Wolitzer, Meg. *This Is Your Life.* 1988; New York: Penguin, 1989.

Index

This index does not include references to material in Notes and Sources.